The Inspector's Guide

Prepare Your
House for Sale

The Inspector's Guide

Prepare Your
House for Sale

BOB REEMSNYDER

THE LYONS PRESS
Guilford, Connecticut

An imprint of The Globe Pequot Press

The Lyons Press is an imprint of The Globe Pequot Press.

10 9 8 7 6 5 4 3 2 1

Printed in the United States of America

Library of Congress Cataloging-in-Publication data

Reemsnyder, Bob.
The inspector's guide—prepare your house for sale / Bob Reemsnyder.
p. cm.
ISBN 1-59228-606-2 (trade paper)
1. Dwellings—Inspection. I. Title.
TH4817.5.R44 2005
643'.12—dc22
2005004478

Contents

Introduction

You are selling your home—or maybe you are just thinking about it and want to be sure that it's in good shape for when you make that decision. Either way, this book is designed to give you a sense of comfort about the condition of your home.

Many people buy a home and overlook regular maintenance issues for so long that they end up turning into major problems. In general, economists recommend that a budget of roughly 1 percent of the value of the home be set aside annually to cover unexpected repairs and annual maintenance. Many homeowners have overlooked maintenance and repairs simply because they were unaware of developing issues. Knowing how to look at your home, where to look, and what to look for, is vital to keeping your home in top shape for your family and to maintaining its value. Cable TV programs such as *Curb Appeal* and *Designed to Sell* have become very popular lately, as they give suggestions and tips on making your house more saleable in the current market.

In today's market, buyers of homes want to feel comfortable that they are getting a quality home that has been reasonably well maintained, so they can protect their investment. As a veteran home inspector, I have seen many deals deteriorate with each issue I point out to a prospective buyer. Some sales are lost because of one major issue, while others are ended due to a long list of minor deferred maintenance items, such as rot found at windows, the need for paint, leaking drains, and debris in the garage, attic, or basement. Often, in leaving an inspection, I wonder why the seller didn't do a few minor things to improve or repair items; I now realize this is often because they were simply unaware of the problems. Frequently, the seller does not know what the inspector will be looking at during the course of the inspection.

The inspection process has become a standard part of the sales contract over the last fifteen to twenty years, though it is not a requirement for a transaction. While each state may have varying regulations, or in some cases, no regulations, this book will help you prepare your home for almost any thorough inspection. This invaluable tool will take you step by step through a self-inspection process, allowing you to critique your home as a potential buyer, or as the buyer's inspector. If used properly, this book will greatly improve your chances of getting the optimal price for your home without delays and additional costs due to a negative inspection report.

You can browse through the entire book, or reference certain parts, including sections on the outdoors, the indoors, and utilities. In addition, we have added some tips for regular maintenance of your home, as well as some unique inspection stories. You will find a checklist at the end of the book to help you stay on task, and maintain a list of items that need attention. Note that the checklist follows the sequence of the book, to make it easy for you to note items that need your attention as you go through this inspection. There is also an informative section on environmental concerns such as asbestos, lead in paint, and radon, well worth browsing through.

When this book is used by both you and your agent, you can brainstorm on how to best prepare for the eventual home inspection, and help eliminate obstacles that may reduce your price, or even delay or kill the sale. But remember, when all is said and done, you still own your home. The final decision is yours to make—whether to repair an item, reduce your price to compensate for issues, or stand firm on your price (risking the loss of the sale).

The Inspector's Guide

Prepare Your
House for Sale

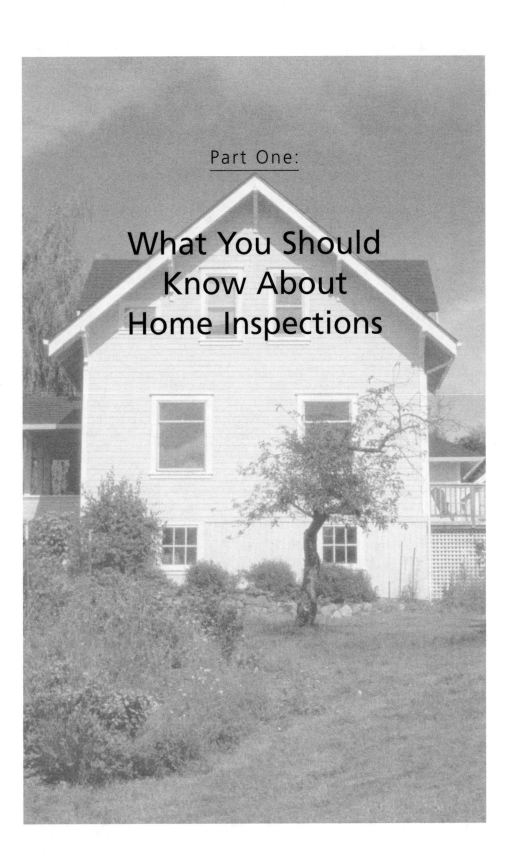

Part One:

What You Should Know About Home Inspections

The Typical
Home Inspection

Upon arrival at your home, an inspector will often pick out details within the first few minutes that most people never notice. He is trained to look for problems and defects that will become major issues (if they are not already). It is likely that he will start the inspection on the outside, checking the outer foundation walls, the siding, windows and doors, roof, chimneys, garage, and decking. The landscaping will also reveal much about the home, so he will be noting problems with that too, such as trees growing too close to the home.

Trees growing too close to a home should be
removed or trimmed before the inspection.

An important part of the inspection, of course, is the basement or crawl space, where any major structural problems might be revealed. A qualified inspector is familiar with standard building practices and the importance of support systems. He will be looking for beams or members that have been altered or display unusual movement or settling, as well as checking the foundation walls for severe cracks or deterioration.

The attic is another important area, as the wood joists or trusses are extremely important to the overall stability of the home. Any cracks in wood members, or beams that have been cut, would be noted as compromising the structural integrity of the home. The inspector will also check out the electrical panel box, the heating and air conditioning systems, and the plumbing components, looking for defects.

Finally, the interior rooms, from the kitchen to the bathrooms to the family room, are also inspected. Your buyer will have a chance to confer with the inspector on the findings, and most good inspectors will take the time to explain the workings of some of the components, such as the boiler or the electrical system. Though the inspection is done to find defects or problems, it is also an opportunity for a new homeowner to learn about the systems of their new home.

The inspector cannot dismantle anything in order to perform the inspection, and he can't spend a great deal of time moving items to access certain parts of the home. While moving a box or two is not considered extraordinary, heavy furniture and crowded storage units will only limit the ability of the inspector to fully view some key areas.

In addition, an inspector is not there as a government official to identify code violations. Though some code requirements may be pointed out for safety reasons (such as spacing between railings of a deck enclosure), many code requirements may not even apply to the home that is being inspected. It is important to note that a house is required to meet certain codes when it is built, but most communities do not require homes to be updated when a new code is enacted. Furthermore, no inspector can be totally familiar with all code requirements, as they are generally different from town to town, and only your local building official, usually at town or city hall, can provide you with the most up-to-date code information.

Finally, a written report will be issued to the buyer by the inspector, which reflects the findings at the inspection. This report usually becomes the document with which a buyer will negotiate further with the seller, based on these findings. Though the job of a home inspector is to find the problems in a home, it is always a pleasure to issue a report to a new home buyer that reflects a home that has been well maintained and is in good condition.

The cost for an inspection varies according to the region, home size, condition, and the inspector you hire. In general, the home inspection, along with typical tests such as water testing, radon testing, and septic inspections, could cost in the range of a thousand dollars. This cost is typically borne by the buyer, though on occasion, a home seller might agree to pay for some of the cost (such as the pump-out fee for the septic system). This cost should not deter anyone from securing a home inspection, as just one major defect could cost far more to address than the combined fees. Though inspections are not mandatory when buying a home, most realtors today will require you to waive your rights to a home inspection if you decide to forego the process.

A thorough home inspection takes a good deal of time—sometimes as long as four or five hours for an average home, if only one inspector is present. Though many home sellers feel it is important to be on hand during the inspection, it is really best for the buyer, the buyer's agent, and the seller's agent to attend the inspection. This will help to speed things along and allow the inspector to interact with his or her client without interruption.

When you use this book to perform your own pre-inspection, plan on taking the time necessary to perform this task. It will certainly take you at least the amount of time that it would take an experienced home inspector, so you might want to do your inspection in stages, such as the outside first, followed by the inside, and then the utilities.

The Well-Informed
Seller and Buyer

Conducting a home inspection is a multitasking project for the inspector, where all parties run the risk of feeling upset, unhappy, or discouraged at the outcome. As you can imagine, a contract that falls apart can be upsetting to the buyer, the seller, and both the listing agent and the buyer's agent. So often, we see the same issues that get in the way of finalizing the sale for home sellers occur over and over again.

It is important to remember that the person buying your home is the one putting down a large amount of money, probably the largest investment of his life. In addition, he is often faced with paying for it over the next thirty years. As inspectors, we are entering your home, looking into every nook and cranny, trying to find any and all defects. It can appear that we are only looking for the bad things about a home. We are also faced with the wide range of reactions that can be brought on by the inspection, including possible interference of the current homeowner, the realtors, and the buyer. It is common for many buyers to experience second thoughts, or "buyer's remorse," during the home inspection. This can negatively impact the process by making the buyer question his decision to buy this particular home. If the inspector keeps finding minor, or major, issues, it only feeds into the buyer's hesitation and can stall, delay, or even halt the process.

Inspectors often test mechanical items that may have not been tested in some time, taking a risk that something might break. Access areas may be covered or difficult to get to. Inspectors may also find themselves in a situation where their safety is at risk, such as in unsafe crawl areas, or structurally unsound areas. And they may be exposed to other unsafe conditions such as live wires, mold, animals and animal waste (from mice, rats, and snakes), protruding nails, broken glass, asbestos, lead paint, carbon monoxide, leaking gas, and so on. Everyone in the inspection process has a different agenda, and for the buyer and seller, it may be their first experience with an inspection. They may not know the responsibility or obligation of each person involved in the process. An agent representing the buyer will usually inform them as to how things will progress as soon as they have an accepted contract, which prevents surprises for the buyer.

So, let's talk about those likely to attend an inspection, and further define each person's obligation. First and foremost, the inspector should be working exclusively for his or her client, the buyer. He should be honest and straightforward, following up with a written report that reflects the condition of the home on the day of the inspection. There should be no other influence upon the inspector during the inspection. The inspector is not obligated to carry on a running conversation with anyone, including the buyer, seller, or agents. There are hundreds of components to look at and report on. The inspector should not discuss his or her findings with anyone but the client, or the client's assignees. Many inspection companies require written permission to copy to a third party, or further discuss with another party. If there are any issues that are to be negotiated within the report findings, they are the responsibility of the buyer or the buyer's assignees, such as the realtor or attorney, to work out with the seller.

The **Not So** Helpful Buyer

Buyers love to open and touch everything they can, to the dismay of most home inspectors. This can include pressing buttons for alarms that are directly linked to emergency services for ill or infirm occupants; opening old and rusty fireplace clean-out doors (emptying the soot all over); struggling with windows that don't want to open (causing them to break); prying open shutters; and various other things. I suppose it's human nature for someone to want to "see" that something really does not work, but often this will cause the actual breakage of an item, leaving the inspector with the task of fixing it.

The seller's agent is working on behalf of the person selling the home, and their presence at an inspection is for the purpose of protecting your property. They will usually provide access on the day of the inspection. They should provide honest and accurate information on your home to the buyer, whether it is negative or positive. They should be well versed in all the components of your home and have a disclosure sheet available, which has been filled out by you. In addition, it is helpful if they provide information on locations of access, and municipal records on the well, the septic locations, etc.

The selling agent should also have keys to all locked areas of the home, including crawl spaces, electrical components, rooms, attics, storage areas, and outbuildings. The seller and their agent should also make sure the utilities are on the day of the inspection. It always amazes me when I show up at an inspection to find that the electricity or water is off. Most inspectors will not—and should not—turn on any utilities (such as water valves), except for normal operating controls such as thermostats, switches, faucets, etc. The general accepted practice for a selling agent is to be helpful, but not follow the buyer and inspector around, allowing private consultations between these two parties.

The buyer's agent should be helpful in representing his or her clients in the sale process, helping with any negotiations concerning the inspection process. It is common for the buyer's agent to be a part of the consultation between buyer and inspector, in order to discuss everything once the report is received.

There are also other players in this process, including appraisers, attorney(s), and possibly a banker or mortgage broker. The appraiser is primarily sent by the bank or mortgage company to determine the dollar value of your home so the bank can feel "secure" with the amount it is lending to your buyer.

It is my belief that if all parties in the transaction acted upon their integrity and honesty, fewer deals would fall apart. There is no perfect home; however, if you follow the suggestions in this book, your home will be in fairly good condition and ready for a successful sale. Most importantly, you should be able to avoid the common pitfalls that often turn buyers away from a property. Whether you own a cottage, mobile home, condo, or large luxury home, there is something for everybody in this book.

Our clients pay hundreds of dollars for us to provide them with much of the information that is included in this text. At the end of the book is a checklist that should be helpful in creating a blueprint to help prepare your home for sale in an organized fashion. Of course, there may be elements unique to your home or local geography that may not be covered in this book. That is why we always recommend that you consult with specialists, such as engineers or local home inspectors, for solving more specific problems, especially when dealing with safety or structural concerns. Good luck in the process of preparing your home for sale, and may you have a smooth and relatively trouble-free transaction.

A General History of Home Inspection

Years ago, most buyers just looked at a property, decided they liked it, put a deposit down, secured a mortgage, and closed on it several weeks later. If they moved into the home and discovered major problems, it was just their bad luck. Issues could include septic systems or wells; structural problems; plumbing, heating, and electrical problems; roofing or siding issues; and doors and windows—and all might be very costly to address. Initially, the idea behind a disclosure by the seller was to provide a totally honest transaction. It soon became evident, however, that surprises could still occur—often because occupants are not always aware of problems in their own home, so they would not know to disclose an issue. People were not aware of the hazards of water contamination, radon gas, radon in water, lead paint, carbon monoxide, lead in pipes, asbestos, aluminum wiring, and product recalls.

About twenty-five years ago, the home inspection industry began to evolve in response to consumer problems. Today, many states have home inspection industry regulations, along with reporting requirements. The home inspection industry has progressed to the point where many inspectors now have high-tech tools, computers, digital cameras, and even Web sites designed to assist the buyer in making this important decision.

The qualifications of inspectors can vary from state to state, depending on the regulations of any given state. Some may be structural engineers, architectural engineers, or builders. Others may have gone through targeted courses that have been designed to train them to assess all components of a home. They may be experts in more than one field. Their credentials can vary, from a high school education to a doctorate, but most have some hands-on experience in the construction industry. Many states now require testing in order to secure an inspection license, and some even require apprenticeship with a licensed home inspector before a license is issued. Both buyers and sellers should become familiar with the regulations pertaining to the home inspection industry in their states.

There are industry standards of ethics that have been developed by professional organizations. The American Society of Home Inspectors (ASHI) is the oldest organization and was the first to establish a set of standards. These standards include reporting requirements, such as using the narrative-style report format, as well as ethical concerns, such as avoiding any conflicts of interest. You can find a full list of the "Standard of Ethics" at www.ashi.org. ASHI-certified inspectors have to meet specific requirements to qualify for the status of full membership, and they must also fulfill yearly credit quotas for continuing education in order to maintain their membership.

The National Association of Home Inspectors (NAHI) is the second-oldest and largest inspection organization. Their standards are similar in nature (promoting professionalism in the field), and they offer information to the general public on the expectations of a thorough home inspection. Their standards of practice and code of ethics are available for viewing at their Web site, www.nahi.org.

Another professional organization, the National Association of Certified Home Inspectors (NACHI), also provides helpful information to inspectors and consumers. Their Web site, www.nachi.org, provides their standards and code of ethics as well.

There are other organizations that may be specific to a particular state or region; for example, CAHI—the Connecticut Association of Home Inspectors—is a subsidiary organization of NAHI, for home inspectors in Connecticut. But all organizations are similar in that the members pledge to abide by standards of practice and a code of ethics. It is important for you as a consumer to know that the inspector you hire is not making money off any jobs he recommends to a friend in the remodeling business. Likewise, you would expect your inspector to give you an unbiased opinion of the condition of a home, and not hold back information because the realtor sends a lot of work his way. I would like to think that thousands of people have avoided injury or death from many of the safety violations discovered by home inspectors. And with this book, I hope that many sellers will be prepared for the home inspection process and prevent the often unnecessary loss of their sale.

Let us take you through a self-inspection of your own home, so you can avoid many of the pitfalls we see in our daily jobs. If you follow this inspection formula, we assure you that you will find many of the items that an inspector would be identifying in his or her report, giving you the opportunity to address them. This is a time-consuming task, particularly if you have not closely examined the condition of your home in the past.

To help you, I have included a home seller's preparation checklist (pages 141–155) that mirrors this inspection process. Make a copy to have on hand while you go through this process to keep track of your findings. You can then organize and prioritize your list once you have completed the inspection. If one section takes longer than you expect, just break up the inspection so you are not overwhelmed. For instance, one weekend, do the exterior sections, and the following weekend, do the basement and attic, finishing up with your interior sections and utilities. Following through on the entire inspection will be well worth your while, as you will reap the benefits once you have a contract. Once you have your completed list of items to address, you can contact specialists to make repairs or improvements as you see fit.

Part Two:

The Outdoors

Exterior Surfaces

Siding

The siding of your home is the outer skin that protects the inner walls. It should be fully weather tight and the finish as attractive as possible for the best presentation. If your home is painted, look for loose or peeling paint, or areas with faded finish or bare spots. Repainting may be necessary and, if done well, may reap a larger profit in your sale. It is best to choose a more popular color for the area you live in. Shocking or unusual colors are not advised, as it may limit those interested in your home right from the first viewing. If your home is older—say, more than forty years old—see the chapter on environmental hazards for information pertaining to lead in the paint. If your home is brick or stucco, look for loose cement or mortar joints, or broken and cracked bricks. If discovered, it may be best to have a professional mason make the repairs.

As you walk around the outside of your home, look closely for any signs of wood rot. Common places that we find wood rot are at the base of the garage door trim, and at the bottom of corner boards where two wood surfaces connect. Using a small screwdriver, probe a suspected area to see if it is soft. The wood should be solid and resist the

The exterior underside of the roof (or soffit) should be checked for rot.

tapping and probing of a screwdriver. If the tool easily penetrates the wood, you have some wood rot, and you want to be sure to note the area so you can repair it in the future. Look up at the fascia board, which is the board behind the gutter, and note the condition of the soffit, the flat part on the bottom of the overhang. Any wood rot you find in these areas can either be repaired or replaced, depending on the extent of the damage.

If you decide to eradicate the rot and use wood filler, it is likely to be noted by a good home inspector, who will then indicate that there is the possibility of further hidden damage. In many cases, the preferred method may be replacement. Depending on your level of expertise, you may be able to make the repairs on your own; or, if you're not confident about doing it yourself, a local carpenter can come to the rescue. If your home is sided with wood shingles, look for loose or missing shingles, or shingles that are badly warped, and plan on replacing them. Wood clapboards sometimes open up or crack, in which case they should be replaced or refastened as necessary. If the home has vinyl siding, look for loose or damaged panels. These can often be replaced or resecured. Sometimes, vinyl siding becomes dirty, covered with growth, moss, or stains. If this is the case, cleaning the surface is recommended. Consider renting a power washer from a rental center to make the job easier, but be sure you are careful with the force of the water. You don't want to use such high pressure that you damage the siding. There are also companies that specialize in power washing.

Loose vinyl siding can be easily replaced.

Windows

Now, check all of your windows. The area around windows is another common area for wood rot that goes unnoticed by many homeowners. Look closely around the

Windowsills are particularly prone to wood rot as
this is an area where water tends to collect.

Check your windows for signs of dried and cracked glazing.
It's time to reglaze them if they look like this.

edges, paying close attention to the area below each window. Look at the sills and the casings (the outer trim). Remember to use your screwdriver to lightly probe these areas. Of course, you will want to replace any cracked or broken windowpanes for a better presentation, so have a tape measure handy for measuring pane sizes. If your windows are single pane, they may have storm windows in colder climates. Check these windows to make sure all of the inserts are installed, and that the screens and inserts move freely. A lubricating oil or silicone spray can sometimes help to free up jammed or difficult panes. Old sashes may need reglazing; that is, replacement of the putty that holds each pane in the sash. When the putty dries up and cracks, the glass pane becomes loose and may rattle or even crack in windy conditions. Be sure to clean out the old, dried putty before reglazing, and finish the process by applying an exterior paint. This keeps the glaze supple for an extended period of time. Remember, sprucing up old windows may help reduce the immediate need for window replacement in the buyer's mind.

If you have Thermopane windows, it's good to check those as well. Thermopane windows are two panes with a narrow space between them. They are factory sealed with a special gas between the panes to keep the glass clear and increase the thermal quality of the window. If the seal has been broken, it may cause "fogging" of the window. This is due to infiltration of air into this space, which allows moisture to dry on the glass. If you note any fogged windows and they are fairly new, they may still be under warranty. Otherwise, contact a glass company for repair options, or consider replacement by a window contractor. You should also make a list of screens that need repair or replacement.

Entrances

All of the entrances to your home should be in good condition, as it makes the first statement in the mind of a buyer about the overall condition of the home. Look at the front and back steps, noting any rotted wood that needs repair, loose or damaged stair treads, and loose or missing railings. If your steps are brick or stone, note any loose bricks, and repair areas that need repointing; that is, fill the grout seams if the concrete is cracking

This set of stairs needs railings, and the lowest rise is too high.

and loose. It may be worthwhile to have a mason do this, as the finished product may be more pleasing to the eye. But wait until you have your final list before calling any specialists like a mason, because you may have more on your list for them to address.

If your steps are higher than two treads, you may want to consider installing railings for safety. Make sure the area around the steps is graded properly away from the steps, and openings are sealed to avoid pests setting up residence under the stairs.

Decks and Balconies

Check your decks and balconies. Replace rotten boards and make sure the railings are secure, not loose or wobbly. Most inspectors will note if there is a space large enough for a child to fall through the railings, so consider upgrading your railings if the spaces are too wide. While each community may have varying requirements, it is a good idea to avoid spaces wider than 3 ½ inches. Most communities have a building inspector for the county or the town who can advise you on the local codes and regulations. Consult the phone directory for government departments to find your local building inspector. Walk the deck surface and fasten any loose boards. If anything is in need of painting or staining, make sure the surface is scraped of loose paint prior to applying the finish. Make sure the deck supports are secure and that they hold the deck as level as possible.

Steps

Stairs and steps are a very important feature, as problems with steps put people at risk. Home inspectors will certainly red-flag stairs that are a safety concern. Things that we

Here's a good example of stairs that would cause an inspector much concern. There are no railings, and the steps themselves are uneven and inconsistently sized.

look for include loose or undersized treads, missing or loose railings, rotted areas, and inconsistent size and spacing of treads (see photo). If they are masonry, check to see if the top is chipped or cracked. Home centers carry resurfacing products to repair these surfaces, including Red Devil House & Home Sidewalk Crack Repair, and QUIKRETE® repair products.

Lighting/Electrical

Exterior light fixtures should be properly secured to a post or the house, and if old and rusty, you should consider replacing them. Exterior outlets should be securely installed, and it is recommended that all exterior outlets be upgraded to Ground Fault Circuit Interrupters, or GFCI outlets (sometimes referred to as GFIs). These outlets serve as protection from severe shock. An electrician can usually upgrade the old outlets as necessary.

Exterior Doors

Take a look at the exterior doors, noting the condition of the surface finish. They may need painting or staining. Check wood doors for rotted areas, and metal doors should have a rust-inhibiting finish applied if you note any rust on the exterior. The weather stripping should be in good condition, without loose or deteriorated strips. Weather stripping replacement on exterior doors is usually a simple matter of taking off the old and reattaching the new, which is readily available in hardware stores or home centers. Check the hinges, tightening if necessary, and make an assessment about the door hardware. If the knob is old, damaged, or corroded, it may be a good time to purchase and install a new entry system. Consider purchasing knobs for all entry doors so you can get keyed-alike hardware. Don't overlook the sliders of your home—do they slide easily? Are there any damaged areas? Clean and lubricate the tracks, if necessary, and make sure the locks work on them. Sliders often have locking systems that are the first to fail, but you can purchase alternative locking systems for sliders, such as a foot lock at the base of a slider, or a bar that can be lowered to prevent entry. Many people will have a dowel or piece of wood cut to size that they place between the slider and wall for security, but this may not be acceptable to your new buyer. On the other hand, it is a minor consideration, so it may be at the bottom of your list of priorities once you are through with the full inspection.

Exterior Plumbing, Wiring, and Pest Problems

Check the hose bibs, or outside faucets, making sure they are not dripping and are operational. A very important issue is the condition of your entry wire on the electrical service. This is the wire that extends from where the power line from the road attaches to your home and goes to the meter. If it is worn or damaged, it is time to call an electrician to do this task, as they will need to contact your power company and coordinate the replacement wire. Note if there are any bees' nests or evidence of carpenter bees. Carpenter bees leave a telltale sign of their work, easily identifiable as you can see in the picture. These should be eliminated as soon as possible. Be careful with these stinging insects, as some people may have severe allergic reactions. Most experts suggest spraying at night. However, if you are nervous about doing this, a professional exterminator should be consulted.

You have now given the exterior of your home a careful inspection, and you probably already have a few things on your checklist to address. Let's continue on with other outside concerns.

These holes are evidence that carpenter bees
have been at work on this house.

Landscaping

Trees and Shrubs

While you are outside of the home, let's take note of the landscaping around the exterior. While shrubs and trees are an asset to the aesthetics of the home, they can also cause problems if not properly maintained. Shrubs should be trimmed back from the home, leaving at least two feet between home and bushes. This helps to keep the home dry, discourages the infestation of wood-boring insects, and the development of wood rot. This job can usually be done without too many specialized tools or talent. Small or large trees growing too close to the home should be removed, preventing roots from growing too close to the foundation, possibly causing cracks and movement. This is usually a job for a professional tree contractor. Overhanging limbs should be trimmed back as necessary, and vines should be removed from all exterior surfaces. The trimming of limbs near power lines should be left to a professional or to the power company, as serious shock could result.

While some think ivy growing on a home is attractive,
it can cause problems and should be removed.

Driveway and Parking

The driveway should be inspected; if hairline cracks exist, there are products at most home centers that can easily be applied to seal these cracks and coat the surface. There are also companies that specialize in driveway repair and surfacing. Check the transition of your driveway to the garage and the road. If there are ruts, dips, or uneven surfaces, they should be altered if feasible, with cement or asphalt patches.

A common problem is the lack of off-street parking, which is highlighted by your parked cars. If parking in your driveway is tight, be sure to park your vehicles elsewhere when showing your house or on the day of an inspection. You'll want to make sure the buyer has a place to park.

Fencing and Walls

If there is fencing or retaining walls, be sure to look over their condition. Is the wood in good condition? If the retaining wall is masonry, look for loose areas, or cracks and voids; it may be necessary to consult with a mason if repairs are necessary.

Grading

The grading of your property can be a potential problem. If the ground slopes toward the house, it encourages puddling of water along the foundation and increases the possibility of basement leakage. Check your basement windows. If they are below grade, window wells will help keep dirt from entering or from obstructing windows. Is the

When soil comes into contact with wood,
termites are often soon to follow.

basement window frame in good condition? Basement windows can be wood, metal, or even vinyl, and you want to make sure the finish is in good condition. Often, metal windows could use a coat of rust-inhibiting paint; wood windows are improved if painted with exterior paint or stain; and vinyl windows may need a good cleaning. Of course, you should replace any broken panes, and make sure the area around the windows has no voids that would allow pest entry.

If there are low areas adjacent to the foundation, backfilling may help direct rainwater away from the home. If there is wood or soil contact around the perimeter of the home, wood-boring insects have an open door. Look for visible mud tubes on the foundation, or along the exposed framing in the basement area (especially the area adjacent to the basement where the front steps are). This would be an indication of subterranean termites. If you see termite evidence, a professional exterminator should be consulted. Termites can do tremendous damage to wood, as they actually ingest the wood, leaving the inner portion substantially weakened. When any evidence of termites is discovered during a home inspection, it will most likely compel the buyer to request treatment or documentation that treatment was recently done. If you have extermination services performed before selling your home, be sure you have your documentation ready for the buyer.

Walkways

Next, look at your walkways. Cracked walkways and deteriorated and uneven surfaces should be repaired to prevent accidents and to give a better presentation. Home

Here is a brick patio that could use
some repair to fix its uneven surface.

centers usually sell products designed to make these types of repairs (visit http://www.quikrete.com/diy/RepairingConcrete.html for an example). Consult with the salesperson for further advice. Often, brick walkways have uneven settling, creating a hazardous condition. Some walkways are bordered with landscape timbers, which might be rotted or poorly installed. Look yours over and make repairs if necessary. This may involve the replacement of part or all of some of the landscape timbers.

Finally, clean the yard for a nice presentation, and by all means, dispose of anything hazardous in your yard, such as old batteries, stored oil, or old car parts. Most towns or cities have special facilities for the disposal of these types of hazardous waste. Get in touch with your local government or town works department to find out more information.

If there are any exterior surface drains, be sure leaves and debris are removed so they drain properly. Take the time to mow the lawn, trim shrubs, shovel walkways in winter, or rake leaves in fall, to give your landscaping the best presentation for the inspection or sale of your home.

Roof and Chimneys

Roof Condition

One of the best ways inspectors determine the condition of a roof is by the age. When checking out your own roof, make sure you inspect it with binoculars, as many roofs are too steep to walk on, and serious injury can result. You can also view areas of your roof from second-story windows, dormers, or balconies (if available) for a close-up view.

Most asphalt shingles will last up to twenty years, and some of the recent architectural shingles are designed to last anywhere from twenty-five to thirty-five years. Wood shingles can last fifteen to thirty years, but that is dependent upon several factors, including the grade of the shingle and the level of maintenance by the owner. Other conditions that affect the aging of all types of roofing material include attic ventilation, the pitch or steepness of the roof, exposure to south and west sunlight, and overhanging growth. When asphalt shingles age, the outer corners tend to curl up, making the shingles appear to have shrunk; the material loses mineral surface, and they become brittle. A good inspector will note these factors in an effort to forewarn the buyer of an upcoming major expense, particularly if there are two layers of roofing material, which means additional cost for the removal of shingles. Unfortunately, if a roof is very old and worn, it might be best to replace it prior to the sale. Your agent can help you decide if the investment in a new roof will bring a better price.

Shingles

If there are shingles that are lifted, it is wise to seal them down, as they are susceptible to heavy winds. In addition, a driving rain might force water up into these small voids. Check the roof surface for cracked or torn shingles (again, you should use binoculars for this). Look for loose shingles, popped nails, and other defects, and have a roofer make necessary repairs.

Wood Roofs

Wood roofs are more difficult to inspect, as the shingles may warp with age in many cases. Sometimes a wood roof may have warped shingles, but they may still perform satisfactorily. Moss-covered shingles can be power-washed if they are not too rotted or soft; sometimes a stiff brush works well on older surfaces. Loose or damaged shingles

Unless you're comfortable with heights and have some experience
in this area, it's best to hire a roofer to fix loose shingles.

should be repaired, and then the entire surface can be coated with a wood preservative. Sometimes the wood is just too rotted, and replacements may be needed. The current rule of thumb on wood shingles is that if more than 10 percent of shingles need replacement, it may be cost-effective to install a new roof. It is often more costly to replace a

Roof valleys are susceptible to the normal wear and tear of sun and rain.
They are often the sites of leakage in the home.

wood-shingled roof with wood shingles, so it may be worthwhile to replace it with a standard asphalt shingle, but check with your real estate professional for advice on this. Depending on the style and age of your home, it may be prudent to stick with a wood-shingled roof.

The crevices found where two rooflines meet are called valleys. Typical materials used to cover the valleys include the shingles themselves, or copper, aluminum, roll roofing, or some sort of sheet stock. Valleys can often develop tears or voids, which, in time, can leak. If you note any of these defects, they should be repaired, for obvious reasons.

Other roofing materials include ceramic tile, which is common in southern climates. When examining tiles for obvious defects, such as cracked, broken, or missing tiles, be sure to use binoculars, as these tiles are slippery and dangerous to walk on.

Flat Roofs

Flat roofs should be examined closely, but be mindful that if you walk on a flat roof, you can cause damage. You will be looking for open voids or seams, blistering of the surface, low areas that allow puddling, and obvious tears. There are coatings that can be applied to roof surfaces with moderate wear that will help rejuvenate the surface. If the surface is too far gone, replacement may be the only option.

Chimneys

Chimneys are often in need of some type of repair, which may go unnoticed by homeowners as they are so high up. They are made of brick, metal, or cement block, and it is again best to use binoculars to look these over. It is preferable to have a lined chimney (in brick and block chimneys, liners are usually made of tile). Insulated metal chimneys

Here is a chimney that needs repointing at the top.

have a double or even triple wall, with some form of fireproofing insulation between them. One of the most common defects found with chimneys is the need for repointing of the brick or block; that is, the cement between the bricks is worn or breaking away at the joints. You want to look for any large cracks along the chimney,

Here you see the crumbling crown of a chimney
with a tile flue, but no cap.

While you're checking your roof condition with your binoculars, be sure to
look for any chimney flashing that has lifted or come loose.

the chimney pulling away from the house, or excessive spalling, which is a deterioration of the surface of the bricks or block. In many cases, the crown, which is the white beveled top covering that protects the brick, may be missing or cracked. In any of these repairs involving masonry materials, it is best to have a mason do the work, as the finished job will not only look nicer, but be properly sealed.

The flashing on the chimney is the transition material between the chimney and the roof that serves to seal the junctions. The flashing material is usually lead, metal, or even copper. Loose pieces of metal flashings should be resecured. Any deteriorated flashing is highly prone to leakage and should be repaired as soon as possible. You will want to check the chimney from inside the attic also, noting any signs of leakage, and making sure that they are not active leaks. Once all repairs are made, you may want to make an effort to clean up or paint over the stains so as not to lose the buyer's potential interest. Many inspectors recommend that a rain cap with screening be installed at the top of the flue, as this protects the inner flue and damper, and can also serve to prevent unwanted visitors and debris inside the flue.

Gutters

While you are looking up, check out your gutters. Debris in gutters can cause ice damming in winter weather. Cleaning the gutters will keep water flowing away from the home. Take a look at where the gutters direct the water; water running out onto a roof may accelerate the deterioration of your shingles. Extend the leaders—which are the pipes that carry the water down—into other gutters, or down to the ground level

A buildup of leaves and other debris can cause ice damming
in your gutters, preventing them from redirecting water
away from the home.

to prevent this. Small concrete pads at the openings of leaders (called splash blocks) can direct water away from the foundation and prevent water ruts caused by the force of the water coming down the leaders. Extensions, which are sections of accordion-like piping, can be fitted at the opening of the downspouts, and bent or stretched out to carry the water well away from the foundation of the house, minimizing the chance of basement leakage. Water running out right next to the house is likely to find some way of getting into the basement area.

Cleaning out gutters is a task that homeowners should perform on an annual basis.

Skylights

Skylights can be another area of concern to both you and your prospective buyer. Defects in skylights include poor flashing, evidence of prior repairs, water stains on adjacent surfaces, cracked glass, or cracks in plastic. Often, if they are skylights that are designed to open, they are not operational due to broken hardware or lack of use. Most skylights have leaked at one time or another. If you have repaired the skylight and it hasn't leaked in a while, sealing adjacent stains with a stain killer and repainting is advised to prevent unwarranted concerns at the inspection.

Ventilation

You should notice a vent pipe coming up out of the roof, usually directly above a bathroom. Vent pipes are necessary so that your toilets, sinks, and other drains flow smoothly and quietly. The boot of the vent pipe is the rubber covering at the base, and should be in good condition. If it is brittle or has obvious voids, it should be sealed or replaced to prevent problems. Unfortunately, the only way to really see it well may be to go up on the roof, which should only be done in safe circumstances or by a roofer, in order to avoid injury.

Your roof may have attic venting, such as roof vents at the peak of the roof, or fans installed in the roof. These should also be examined to be sure that they are properly sealed and no voids exist.

The Garage

The importance of a safe garage cannot be underestimated, as it usually houses gas-driven items such as automobiles and yard equipment, carrying with it the potential of fire danger. Detached garages pose less of a risk, but should be inspected for many of the same components. First, you want to clean your garage of any debris and stored items, so you can adequately inspect for any improvements you can make. Be sure to get rid of unnecessary hazardous stored items or debris, such as paint cans and old oil containers. This kind of hazardous debris can effectively stop a buyer in his tracks.

Walls

If your garage is attached to your home or tucked under a living area, you want to be sure that there is proper fire protection on common walls. The walls that are adjacent to the living space should be sheetrocked with ⅝-inch, fire-rated drywall and coated with at least one coat of tape at the seams. Look for any voids in the drywall as they will cause a breach in the fire structure, and if noted, they can be patched with taping compound. The door to the interior of the home should be a fire-rated metal door, with no glass installed. Hollow-core and solid-wood doors do not meet these safety requirements. However, it may not be cost-effective to replace them unless the buyer or their inspector presses the issue. The floor of the garage should also drop down at least four inches, as this will prevent gasoline or oil spillage from spreading into the living space. Obviously if your home does not meet this feature, an inspector may only note the fact that when the home was built, it was not a requirement. Typically, homes built before 1975 may not have these features. If it is cost-effective—in the range of a few hundred dollars—you may want to consider adding these features for your own safety, as well as improving the sales appeal of your home. Newer homes are likely to meet these safety requirements, and most inspectors would likely call it a defect if they don't.

Automatic Garage Door Openers

One of the most common defects found in the garage is the lack of a working safety feature on the automatic garage door opener. The opener should be properly adjusted so that if the door is blocked by something, it will automatically reverse. Early models had only a pressure sensor, which would cause the door to reverse if resistance was met when lowered. The newer models also have a sensor beam set at a low level, which would detect a small child or animal before the door actually touches them, causing the door to reverse. A defect or improper installation puts children, animals, and even cars at risk. If the unit only stalls, it would still be considered a defect, as the entire door needs to reverse for proper safety requirements. Homeowners should test both the pressure sensor and the beam sensor regularly to be sure that no harm comes to loved ones. Manually operated doors should open and close smoothly and without too much effort, and they should certainly not slam down. Sometimes the springs or cables may need adjustment or replacement, but if you are unfamiliar with garage doors, consult with an overhead door company, as some of the mechanisms can be dangerous, particularly the springs.

Doors

Check the finish on the doors, whether wood or metal, for any deterioration, rot, or defects. Be sure to take a look at the bottom gasket and the sides for openings where mice and drafts can enter. If the door is wood and damaged, replacement of affected panels may be needed. Metal doors may have dents or areas that have rusted over time, and may also need painting or replacement. The overhead door closers should have a dedicated outlet, without the use of extension cords.

Wiring and Plumbing

Now look around the garage for hanging wires, open splices, open junction boxes, and abandoned wires. If noted, an electrician should repair them. Replace any broken cover plates on switches or outlets as needed. How is the lighting fixture? If it is broken or the light is out, it should be replaced. If there is plumbing present, make sure your heat source is working properly to prevent freezing pipes.

Stairs and Floors

If stairs are present, you will want to examine the treads to be sure they are secure, as well as the railing. Check the floor slab for cracks; if numerous and large, it may be wise to seal them. And if the floor is wood, be sure that the structural integrity of the wood is intact, particularly if cars are going to be stored on this surface.

Other Structural Components

Finally, look over the structural items; how is the framing next to the garage doors? Look over the garage door trim and jamb for wood rot. This is a common area that is prone to rot or wood-boring insect activity. Check the board or plate that touches the floor for rot or insect damage. These are areas that commonly show evidence of deterioration, yet go unnoticed by most homeowners. If there is a window in the garage, make sure it is in operational condition. Many homeowners overlook garage window maintenance. Swing doors to the exterior (known as access doors) should also be evaluated for obvious defects, and repaired. Some homes have furnaces, boilers, or oil tanks located in the garage. If this is the case, there should be protective devices such as metal posts installed to help prevent damage to them if a car rolls forward.

At this point, you have completed looking at all aspects of the outdoors section of the inspection, and should have an idea as to your fix-it needs. You should also have a good idea as to the time commitment required for this self-inspection, and should decide whether to continue with the inspection, or wait until another day to go on.

Part Three:

The Indoors

The Basement

The basement is of great importance for an inspector, as the observable structural components of the house are located here, and it often houses the major mechanical components, such as boiler, furnace, and water heater. One of the main concerns for a buyer is leakage, dampness, or standing water. Any of these conditions can cause excessive moisture, which in turn causes wood rot and promotes mold growth, a condition that has become a major health concern in recent years.

Water Seepage

When you first enter your basement, note any standing water or possible water stains on the floor or creeping up the walls. Pay attention to the smell of the basement. Does it have a musty smell? Remember, a potential buyer will notice smells that you may have become immune to.

If your basement has any evidence of water seepage, look around the exterior of the building, checking for dirty or clogged gutters or disconnected downspouts. Downspouts should extend away from the building to prevent water infiltration. Are there any low areas next to the foundation that collect water? Is water seeping around any foundation protrusions such as waste pipes, water supply inlets, or cracks?

Very often, water seepage in basements can be corrected by addressing some of these relatively minor issues. Clean the gutters, making sure that the downspouts are not blocked, and extend the downspouts to discharge *away* from the house. Most home centers have accordion-style extenders that fit nicely over the end of downspouts.

Cracks in Foundation

If there are cracks in the slab or walls of your foundation, there are several companies that specialize in sealing foundation cracks. Check your yellow-pages directory under "Basement Waterproofing" or "Contractors" for companies in your area.

There are also products available at home centers for the handyman, such as:

- **Hydraulic cement:** This product requires chiseling a channel in the crack to apply. See http://www.quickrete.com/catalog/HydraulicWater-StopCement.html for more information.

- **Resilient caulks:** These products are easy to apply. See http://www.quickrete.com/catalog/GrayConcreteRepair.html.

- **Epoxy sealants:** These products are good for both waterproof and structural repairs. See http://www.mountaingrout.com/ for examples of these products.

It is a good idea to seal these cracks even if they are not a structural concern, as the buyer can panic and worry that it is the result of settling.

If the evidence of seepage is from an old problem, and your basement has not leaked recently, be sure to replace or repair stained sheetrock or rotten wood. There are products, such as basement patch and paintable sealants on the market that will seal a stain prior to painting, preventing the stain from "bleeding through" the newly painted surface. Sometimes it may be necessary to totally remove drywall if it is saturated and warped by water.

Electrical Fixtures

You will want to check out the electrical fixtures and wiring in the ceiling, as well as in the walls. Very often, basements will have open junction boxes; that is, splices that are not in a junction box and fitted with a cover. You may also find abandoned wires, loose boxes, dangling wires, and broken outlets. An electrician should be consulted if these problems exist.

Knob and tube wiring might be found if your home is very old, or antique. Note the picture of knob and tube wiring on this page. If this wiring is currently being used, it might be time to update the wiring. If you leave some of the old knob and tube wiring for sentimental reasons (for some, it is a conversation piece), be sure that it is

Knob and tube wiring is often found in older homes. If it is still in use, it should be assessed and updated by a qualified electrician.

clearly disconnected and not in use and point that out to the inspector beforehand. Be sure that the lightbulbs in the basement work, and replace if necessary.

Plumbing

You should now check out the plumbing. Are there any leaks, drips, or corroded areas on the waste lines? The waste lines are the larger diameter piping, usually 1½ inches to 4 inches in diameter, in cast iron or PVC (polyvinyl chloride—the hard white plastic pipe). Be sure to run the water in all the bathrooms and the kitchen while you are checking this area, or prior to doing this. It is common to discover leaks in pipes that serve a rarely used bathroom or Jacuzzi. Next, examine all the water lines, otherwise known as the supply piping, for leaks or drips. These would be the smaller diameter pipes (usually ½- to ¾-inch) in copper or translucent white PVC. Pay careful attention to valves, as they may have developed drips.

If your home has a well, there should be a tank called an expansion tank, which should also be checked for drips or even rust holes. If any leaks are detected and you don't feel comfortable repairing them yourself, consult with a plumber.

Basement Windows

The basement windows should be repaired if the glass is broken or cracked. Tighten up hardware on the windows so they work nicely and provide a tight seal. If they are dirty, it might be a good time to clean the glass.

Hatchway

If you have a hatchway leading to the basement, look at the outer surface finish. If it is metal and rusted, it should be scraped and painted with a rust-inhibiting paint. Sometimes

A rusty hatchway can be a real turnoff to a buyer and can
be easily scraped and painted in an afternoon.

small holes can be patched with metal filler if the door is in very rough shape, but often replacement may be the only option. Check the hardware on the hatchway to see that it is working properly. Spraying with a lubricant sprayer, such as WD-40, will improve the hardware functions. If the hatchway is made of wood, check for rotted areas and repair boards as necessary. Be sure the wood is scraped, and painted with an exterior paint to preserve the wood. More often than not, the access has stairs within the hatchway. You will want to examine them for loose or damaged treads. If a secondary door is at the base of this stairway, look at the bottom for water, or rotted and damaged areas.

Basement Stairs

The basement stairs leading from the basement to the house proper should also be secure, with railings on both sides. The spaces between each rail should be small enough to prevent a child from slipping through or getting wedged. The railings should be secure, sturdy, and safe in design.

The treads and risers should be consistent and of a normal configuration. When a stairway is constructed, it is important to have each tread height be the same, as we tend to "anticipate" our next step. When walking up a flight of stairs, our brain—an amazingly precise computer—automatically calculates the step height, and we raise our foot to that height. If one step is just a quarter-inch higher, most people will stumble on that step. If your home has a stairway with this inconsistency, you have probably adapted to it over time, and never miss that step; however, you may have noticed that your guests often stumble coming up. This idiosyncrasy should be corrected before someone trips and gets hurt. Stairs are one of the main causes of accidents in a home.

As with all other stairways, these basement stairs should have railings that are secure, safe, and spaced properly.

Structural Components

Now let's take a look at the structural components of the basement. You are going to look at all the wood beams, along the perimeter and in the center. Look for rotted wood, or wood damaged by insects. One of the typical areas is in the basement floor framing, adjacent to where the front or back steps are. As mentioned earlier, termites create mud tubes when infesting a home; if you notice any of these tubes, an exterminator should be consulted immediately. While removing the tubes may take away the evidence of termites, it will do nothing to terminate the activity if they are alive. If you have already had your home treated for termites, be sure to have the documentation readily available. This documentation is the proof that your home was treated and may not need further treatment. If you discover damage, you may want to have it repaired now. A buyer gets very nervous when damage is discovered, as there is always the possibility of hidden damage, so it's best to have a contractor or carpenter properly repair the damage ahead of time.

Termite mud tubes should be checked by an exterminator to
determine if the termites are active.

Termites and Carpenter Ants

Very often, termite and carpenter ant colonies will "swarm" when the colony has reached a certain size. Large numbers of these pests suddenly appear at windows and doors of the home, as they leave the colony in search of a new location. First, you want to determine if they are termites or carpenter ants. Termite swarmers are ¼ to ⅜ of an inch long and black in color. Their bodies do not have a narrow waist and the antennae are straight, not bent. If wings are present, they have many veins, and the pair on each side is equal in size. Carpenter ant swarmers are slightly larger—½ to ¾ of an inch in length, and they are also black. Their bodies have a constricted waist, dividing the body into two sections, and their wings have fewer veins. The rear, or back wing is smaller than the forward wing. Termites ingest wood, causing tremendous damage, while carpenter ants will excavate moist wood for nesting, thereby causing less damage.

The southern states also have the Formosan termite, which has been known to destroy massive amounts of wood and is an expert at hiding. The tunnels they create can stretch three hundred feet. These termites can also be transported from one location to another in old wood products.

Florida has the dampwood termite. Unlike the subterranean termite, it does not require any contact with the soil. These termites live in undecayed wood with low moisture content. Dampwood termite colonies have the queen, the larvae, the soldiers, and once strong in numbers, the alates. These are soldiers that molt into flying insects that go out in search of new locations for colonization. The alates are strong fliers and, as nocturnal flying insects, are attracted to lights. Porch lights, indoor lights, and video monitors often lure them inside, especially when doors and unscreened windows are opened.

Foundation Walls

Your foundation walls will be made of block, poured cement, or even stone with concrete filler. They should be fairly straight, without bowing in or out. Keep in mind that any noticeable deflection into the basement or to the outside may indicate some soil movement, resulting in compromising the structural integrity of your home. If you notice unusual movement such as this, it might be time to consult with a mason and/or a structural engineer. If your home is an antique home—that is, over one hundred years old—it may be common to see some movement, though it may still warrant the advice of a contractor or engineer. Your stone foundation may have voids between the stones and will need occasional repointing, which involves the filling of these spaces with concrete (the same holds true of your block foundation). Sometimes these cracks will allow water penetration, so note the evidence of water and weigh the pros and cons of having this addressed by a professional basement sealing company. If you are unsure, or unfamiliar with period building techniques, it is wise to have the counsel of an expert on antique homes and building practices. Keep in mind: It is better to have major problems resolved prior to the home inspection—or at the very least, have readily available solutions at hand—than to have the home inspector be the first to identify potential problems.

The basement slab or poured floor is usually not a structural component. However, many inspectors may recommend that cracks be sealed in order to prevent future water penetration.

Insulation

If your home is newer or has been renovated, insulation may be present in the basement ceiling. Look for missing areas of insulation, or even damaged areas. It is not uncommon to see insulation that has evidence of rodent nesting. While to many this may be a typical occurrence, some home buyers may feel uncomfortable with this.

Sawdust on an area of the insulation could indicate the presence of carpenter ants. Technically, this is called ant frass, which is the by-product of carpenter ants at work. On the other hand, it could also be regular sawdust if someone has used a saw and not cleaned up. Either way, it is better to clean up this dust—but if you see living (or dead) large black ants nearby, an exterminator should be consulted. The discovery of carpenter ants may also indicate a moisture problem in that area, meaning rotted wood is usually not far away (thus the sawdust!).

Sump Pump

If your basement has a sump pump, make sure it is operational and that the discharge is at least fifteen feet from the outside foundation.

• • •

You have now performed a fairly complete inspection of your basement, and you are ready to address the repair items that you have on your list.

Crawl Spaces

———————

While a basement allows a person to comfortably walk around in the lowest level of a home, a crawl space is considered any space that does not allow you to stand straight up, and is usually less than six feet high. Many crawl spaces are just what the name implies—an area accessible only by crawling on your belly around the interior. Crawl areas beneath a home can be the most distasteful part of any inspection, particularly if they have not been well maintained. If you have a crawl space, it is essential for the successful sale of your home that you attend to some basic issues that may turn into major problems if not addressed. The first thing you want to note is your access area; while some have access from the interior, many crawl spaces are only accessible from the outside. Note the condition of the access area. The access door to the crawl space should be vermin- and weatherproof, and easy to open and close. If it is complicated to get to, it may make a buyer hesitant. Installing hinges and a latch may be a minor investment, but can reap major benefits. Also, be sure that your access is not blocked by debris or insulation.

Once you have access, using a bright flashlight, observe the condition of the interior, and determine how you will move around the space. If you will be crawling or creeping on your stomach, you may want to put on a protective suit, gloves, knee pads, and even a respirator. Crawl spaces can be dangerous places filled with vermin, insects, and filth, so these protective precautions may be a good choice. Cleaning out the debris in a crawl space is important, as old wood encourages termites. Some of the loose wood debris in a crawl space may not even be part of the house proper, but if termites are found in this wood, treatment by an exterminator may be recommended to your buyer. Remember, termites can do amazing damage to wood! The removal of this debris can save you thousands of dollars, and also assists the inspector, as an injury can occur if he has to move your stuff out of the way.

Ventilation

Once inside the crawl space, you should have a good idea about the humidity in the area, but look for ventilation concerns. Poor ventilation will cause havoc down below—damaging insulation, causing deterioration to foundation walls, and rotting and weakening the floor structure. Note the ventilation in the crawl space and if it is set for the appropriate season. If vents or windows are closed up, they should be opened in late spring to early fall. The vents should be covered with screening and wire mesh to prevent unwanted tenants. Close the vents in winter to keep the area warmer. If the crawl space has a vent fan, be sure that it is working properly and that the plug wires are in good condition. You will want to note if the laundry vent goes through the crawl space, making sure it is securely connected with no voids in the length of it. If plastic, consider replacing it with a metal flex for your own safety.

Wood Rot

Using a screwdriver, probe a sampling of the floor joists. If they are soft or rotted, a carpenter should be consulted. Replacement may be necessary, or in some cases repairs such as sistering a joist (adding another wood member to the side of the problem joist to make it stronger) may be the best option. Pay careful attention to areas below the kitchen and baths, where water leakage would be most likely. If leakage has occurred, the subflooring or joists could also be damaged. As always with any exterior components, you will want to look for mud tubes on foundation walls, support posts, or framing, and call an exterminator if this evidence of termites is discovered.

Insulation

One of the more common problems we find in crawl areas is the incorrect installation of insulation. When installing insulation, the paper or foil side should be facing the interior of the house; thus, it should not be visible from underneath. Homeowners will often install insulation in an old home after purchase, and keep the paper facing them so they can staple it to the joists. Many don't even know that this is

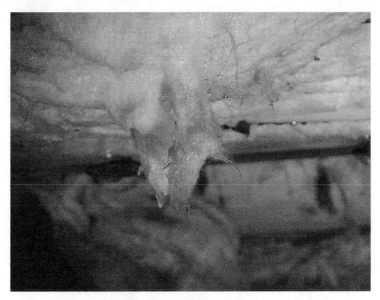

Insulation that has been improperly installed can invite
excessive moisture and cause wood rot.

backwards, but when installed this way, insulation can trap moisture within the joist cavity and cause wood rot. If any of the insulation has fallen, or you notice loose pieces, they should be reinstalled as necessary. If any of the insulation is wet, it should be replaced.

Installing insulation is usually not a fun job, as fiberglass can be itchy to the skin and not good to breathe in. If you are doing the work yourself, wear a protective suit along with gloves and a respirator. There are insulation companies that specialize in this type of work, and it may be well worth hiring one to do the job. Holes in the insulation, or yellow stains on plastic, can be an indication of mice. These are nervous creatures and typically hide if noises are evident. If you notice this evidence, clean the feces from the floor and be sure to wear appropriate mouth and nose protection, as respiratory infection could occur. While mice are a common problem in most homes (the evidence of tiny black droppings will readily indicate mice), larger droppings may indicate a bigger problem, such as rats, squirrels, or other wild animals. If there are live animals present, a company that specializes in animal removal should be contacted. You may have to contact your wildlife agency (check your government listings) to find a company or individual who is licensed to trap and remove wild animals.

Moisture

Most inspectors will note if a dirt floor is present and will recommend installing a moisture barrier. For every 1,000 square feet of uncovered soil in a crawl space, about 5 gallons of moisture evaporates into the air every twenty-four hours. That is over 1,800

Lally columns may be either repainted or replaced, depending on the extent of the rust.

gallons of water a year, and can be a major contributing factor to mold, rot, and insect infestation under a home. The ideal floor in a crawl area is a poured concrete floor, but a sheet of plastic should be installed if it is just a dirt floor, to help contain ground moisture. Black plastic, 6 mil thick, is better than clear as it prevents the transmission of light through to the soil, which can result in organic growth. Adjoining sheets should overlap at least one foot and the edges could be secured with items such as bricks or concrete blocks to hold them in place.

If the area is moist or wet, the steel support columns are prone to and may, in fact, show signs of rusting, particularly at the base. Painting the metal with rust-inhibiting paint may help. If the columns are too badly rusted, replacements may be needed. If the posts are wood, inspect for rot, again, especially at the base. Finally, have someone flush all the toilets and run water in the sinks and tubs while you are down there listening for leaking pipes—both in the supply or drainpipes. A leaky waste pipe can quickly turn off a prospective buyer, so have a plumber fix any leaks, but first mark them well to save the plumber from having to look around for the leaks.

Heating and Wiring

In northern climates, inspectors will look for a heat source to help prevent pipes from freezing. Sometimes the furnace or boiler is in a crawl space where it is sufficiently closed to the outside elements, or you may have heating tapes on your pipes. If you have been using heating tapes, check their condition and replace any necessary strips. You should also note the condition of the wiring, looking for open junction boxes, hanging or terminated wires, frayed or rusted wiring, etc. If any of these conditions are discovered, an electrician should be consulted. Remember, you don't want to be responsible for anyone, including yourself, coming in contact with a live wire. Open splices should be installed within junction boxes, with cover plates. Loose and dangling wiring should be stapled up; rusty BX wires may need replacement.

Using your flashlight, look around and make sure none of the beam supports have settled or fallen over; if they have, consult with a carpenter. Be sure to look for any obvious structural concerns like broken joists. If the home has forced-air heat, look over the condition of the ductwork. Disconnected ducts should be reattached, and damaged ducts replaced. All heating ducts should be securely hung with proper strapping and sealed tightly at the joints. Also note any duct wrappings that might contain asbestos (see photo on page 88). Asbestos is considered a hazardous material in certain circumstances; be sure to refer to the chapter on environmental hazards for more information about this and other dangerous substances.

In general, replace any broken glass in the windows, and paint the frames where needed. Check for voids or light coming through foundation walls, as this allows mice or animals to enter. Older homes may have piled-up stones as part of the foundation, and you want to note any areas that look loose or may have shifted.

Slab on Grade

Some homes have no basement or crawl space, and the first floor is a poured concrete slab. This condition does limit what an inspector can inspect, which may be to your benefit. However, there are still some things you can look for that would cause concern to an inspector. Look for any substantially raised areas of concrete when walking on anything covering it, such as carpet, vinyl, or wood floors. These may indicate a cracked and raised slab, which may only be repairable by removing carpet or flooring. If the floor is ceramic tile, large cracks may also indicate the same condition. You will have to make the decision whether to sell your home with the cracks or pay a concrete floor company to make repairs. The cost of the repair will depend upon several factors, such as the size and depth of the crack, as well as the need to remove and reinstall any or all of the floor covering. Some of these decisions may rest on the value of your home, the area, land costs, etc. If you are trying to get top dollar for your home, and it is in a luxury home area, it may be important to perform some of these repairs in order to reach your sales goal. If your home is valued at under $100,000, it may not be worth doing much with it.

Another area to look at is the heating, supply, and waste pipes embedded in floors, and entering the slab. Look for evidence of water leakage, either bubbling around the entrance points or excessive moisture in one area. If you note any obvious conditions, a plumbing contractor should be consulted.

The Attic

A full examination of the attic is important, as this area below the roof should keep the home watertight and help maintain even temperatures. Your first task may be to clean out the closet where the hatchway or stairway to the attic is located. In rarely used attics, a hatchway may be in a closet full of stored items or hanging clothes. If your home is under contract and an inspection is scheduled, it is advisable to clear out the area to make it easily accessible. In so doing, you are not only preventing damage to your belongings—you are also speeding up the inspection process.

Once in the attic, move any stored boxes that are in the main walkway to make it easier to get around. While some attics are completely covered with subflooring, many have no walkways, just insulation between each of the ceiling joists. Others have decking on just part of the attic. Be sure to walk on the areas with decking only, as the insulation is generally laid on top of the sheetrock below. This is not designed to hold the weight of a person, so you will fall right through! If your attic has loose planks on which to walk, you might want to secure them, or add a few more to allow enough

Blown-in insulation has been used in this attic.
It is easier to use in tight spaces than rolled insulation.

space to maneuver around the attic. Remember, the buyer will likely check out the attic with the inspector, and in the excitement can easily step in the wrong place.

Insulation

Insulation in the attic might be rolled insulation or loose, blown-in insulation. You might need to rearrange any loose insulation, filling in areas where insulation is missing. Check to make sure the bathroom fan exhaust goes to the exterior, either through soffit vents (which is the flat overhang at the bottom edge of the roof) or a gable vent (at the peak of one of the end walls). If the bath fan vents into the attic, it can cause moisture buildup and damage to the sheathing over time. You also want to make sure that all the vents are open and that they have not been sealed up or had insulation, sheathing, or sheetrock installed over them.

Ventilation

Proper ventilation in an attic is essential, as without it, your roofing material will age quicker. You may get a buildup of moisture and possibly even a problem with mold. Some homes have a ridge vent (you will see a slot cut at the peak) and/or soffit vents (you should see light along the perimeter). If you have soffit vents, you want to be sure that the insulation is pulled back so as not to block the vents. If your attic has a venting fan, be sure that it is working properly. Many attic fans are thermostatically controlled, so the homeowner does not have to turn it on in hot weather and off as the temperature goes down. If yours is a manual fan, you might want to look into upgrading it to a thermostatically controlled unit for convenience. This would be installed by an electrician, and should cost

These roof trusses show that this attic has poor ventilation, which has led to the growth of black mold.

under $200. Take a close look at the roof sheathing. If it is moist or black, this could be an indication of a ventilation problem, and a roofing contractor should be consulted.

Here is an example of "high hat" lighting that is hazardous because of the close proximity of the insulation surrounding it.

Wiring

As in all other areas of the home, you want to note any electrical concerns. Of course, if you find any, they should be repaired. If your home has "high hat" lighting present—that is, fixtures protruding up into the insulation—they should have a stamp at the side, which would tell you if it is a fixture designed to avoid hazards due to insulation installed right up against it. If you cannot find this label, or are unsure, it is wise to trim the insulation away from the fixture for safety.

Structural Conditions

The rafters are the long beams that go from the peak of the roof down to the soffits, or bottom edge of the roof. These should be in good condition, so examine carefully for any cracked or broken members. Often, rafters can be sistered if they are cracked—that is, another member is bolted or nailed to the side of the member for the full length. Truss repairs may be more difficult, and a builder familiar with this type of repair should be consulted.

Now, turn off the lights and note if you can see any light from the exterior; of course, this has to be done in the daylight to be effective. If light is visible, roof repairs should be done. Check around the chimney for any signs of leakage, and be sure to have them repaired if they are active leaks.

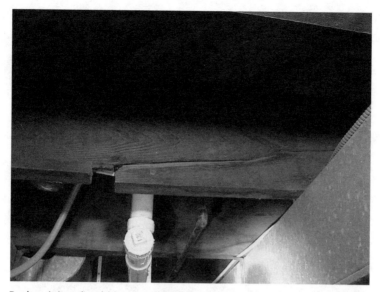

Broken joists should be examined and repaired. Consult with a builder
if you are unsure how to fix this important structural concern.

Stairs

Finally, make sure the access area is in good condition. If stairs are present, do you need railings around the top to prevent someone from falling into the stairwell? If a drop-down stair is installed, is it safe? Look for broken pieces or loose hardware. And if it is just an access cover, is it in good condition? Many attic hatch covers are fitted with some type of insulation to keep the extreme temperatures of the attic out of the living space.

Fireplaces and Woodstoves

To many people, a beautiful fireplace is the focal point of a home, as it is where the buyer often envisions his or her most memorable family gatherings. You will want to enhance the positive aspects of your fireplace, while minimizing concerns.

Fireplace Maintenance and Repair

If you have burned a lot of wood and have not recently had your chimney professionally cleaned by a chimney sweep, it is recommended that you do so. Take a good look at the fireplace from afar. Is it clean and appealing? Move up closer and check the outer areas. You will want to note if there are any cracks in the brick, stone, or concrete above the firebox (the interior section of the fireplace). While many chimneys have some minor cracking, some cracking may be an indication of settling, or movement of the chimney. Minor cracking might be one or two cracked bricks that have not separated, or some small cracks in the concrete around the bricks—often referred to as "step cracking." On the other hand, if the cracks are long and continuous through several bricks or stones, it might be time to consult with a mason, as this can be a major concern to a buyer.

Check that the mantle is in good shape and not pulling away from the wall. Look at the hearth for any cracks or loose bricks. Of course, repair these where you can. These loose bricks can sometimes be resecured with contact cement, but read the label on the product you use to be sure it will adhere to cement or brick materials. Look around where the hearth meets the firebox; note if the raised hearth is pulling away from the fireplace. Also check where the fireplace meets the wall. If there is evidence of separation, again, it would be wise to consult with a mason, who may be able to just fill the voids with cement (also known as repointing).

You will want to clean out any ash or debris from the firebox, so you can see the floor, as well as the back and side walls. Check for cracks, loose mortar, or voids between bricks. Minor hairline cracks are usually okay, but if you see any openings in the concrete, you should again consult with a mason. Check the damper—the metal "flap" that opens or closes to allow air flow to the flue—to be sure that it operates freely and is not jammed with debris above it. It is common to find some rust on a damper, but if it is substantially rusted, and affecting the operation, you might want to have it replaced. With a flashlight, take a look up into the flue, which is the "tunnel" going up through the chimney. Of course, it will likely be black, but do you see any built-up creosote flakes on the sides? This will appear as shiny layers of black ash pulling away from the sides of the flue. This is a good indication that it is in need of a cleaning. You will want to note if there are any voids between the bricks or stones and consult with a mason if you notice any. If there are glass doors, check that they operate freely, and spray a lubricant on moving parts where needed.

Woodstoves

Woodstoves can be problematic if incorrectly installed. They should have a fire-preventive surface such as bricks, slate, or insulated metal above, below, and around them, or there should be a distance of at least eighteen inches from any combustible surface. It is important that the flue pipe is intact with secure connections. If you note substantial rust on the flue pipe, it is a good idea for your own safety to have it replaced, or examined by a qualified professional. You can always consult with your local fire marshal through your town or county government for advice on the local codes governing the installation of woodstoves. If you intend to remove your woodstove, it is best to either do it before you list your home, or be sure to make this known to your real estate agent. By all means, once a stove is removed, be sure to properly seal the flue opening for safety reasons.

If your house is under contract, it is a good idea to refrain from having a fire right before the inspection so that the inspector is able to give your fireplace a good rating. And be sure that your firewood is not stored improperly in a garage or against the house. This encourages insect and ant infestations within the home, creating more problems for you. You don't want to have to pay for exterminating services for the buyer, so be sure to keep wood stored separately from the home.

The Laundry Room

Vents

The laundry room is a functional area with many mechanical systems—meaning more that can go wrong! One of the most common defects noted in inspectors' reports deals with unsafe, plastic dryer vent discharge hoses. Lint builds up on the inside of a vent and the dryer coils are hot enough to ignite this highly flammable material, putting occupants at risk. If your vent hose is plastic, it should be replaced with a flexible metal, fire-rated foil hose or rigid metal discharge. The discharge should continue to the exterior of the home, and not into a basement, crawl space, attic, or garage. The vent cover at the exterior should be in good condition and not damaged or clogged with built-up lint. You can use a vacuum cleaner for any accessible areas to clean out some of the lint.

Wiring

Check your electrical outlets for your washer and dryer. The receptacle for the electric dryer is typically high-voltage 220, so it is very important that it is installed securely and is not hanging down. If your dryer is a gas dryer, you want to be sure that the gas lines are intact and secure.

Water

Having water-supply and waste lines behind appliances means that when leaks occur, it may be some time before you become aware of a problem. Whether selling your house or not, you should check your laundry area on a regular basis to prevent unwanted damage to floors and ceilings. Many laundry rooms today are equipped with the multi-port system, which keeps the water-supply lines and waste lines in one watertight area. Others have the typical throw valves—with a lever that goes up and down and simultaneously turns on both hot and cold—or rotary valves, which have a knob to turn for each faucet attached to the wall. No matter what your feed-line system is, you want to be sure that the water-supply valve is leak free.

The washer hoses should be intact—not rotted, old, or corroded. Your waste-discharge hose should also be checked for deterioration, and be sure that there are no kinks in the line, preventing adequate drainage to your waste pipe. Many homes with a laundry room on the second floor have a drip pan beneath the washer, in case of overflow. This is a great preventive measure to avoid costly damage to the rooms below. If your washer discharges to a laundry sink, make sure it is draining freely.

Finally, be sure that all clothes are cleared away for showings and inspections, and that the light fixtures work properly.

Bathrooms

————

Your bathrooms can be one of the biggest selling points of your home, or your greatest detractor, depending on their condition. While usually the smallest rooms in the house, bathrooms have many components, and you want to be sure they are all working properly.

"Anyone Know a **Locksmith?**"

On one inspection, a seller neglected to inform the agent that the second-floor bathroom door lock would stick in the closed position. A locksmith had to be called, yet he was still unable to open the door without destroying the lockset, which was an expensive antique reproduction. A well-placed ladder and open window saved the day, and the door was successfully opened from the inside. As it turned out, the lockset was improperly installed.

Toilet

Of course, the first thing is to be certain your toilet flushes properly and has no leaks. Check the feed line for any signs of leakage, as well as around the base of the toilet. At the same time, be sure that the toilet is securely set in place and does not rock back and forth. If your toilet is loose at the base, it may be wise to replace the wax seal, and re-seat the unit. Loose toilets are not only prone to leakage, but can cause cracking of the ceramic tiles in the floor. If your toilet is cracked, or badly chipped, it is time to invest in a new model.

Sink Area

You also want to be sure that your sink area is in fairly good condition, checking that the countertop is dry with no water damage, that the sink is well seated in the countertop, and that the whole unit is securely attached to the base. A pedestal sink should also be securely seated in the base. If there are any signs of rust, or damage to the sink (such as cracks or chips), there are products that will take out some of these stains and fill in small chips. Check your hardware store for stain removers such as CLR (for calcium, lime, and rust), Lime-Away, and porcelain filler products. Run the water and check to see if the drain holds water. It may be that the drain mechanism only needs a small adjustment, and now would be a good time to do that. While the water is running, be sure that the faucet does not leak, or that it does not drip when turned off.

Look over the cabinet for any problems with the surface, drawers, or doors. Small adjustments now can make the inspection process go more smoothly later. If the inside of the cabinet shows evidence of prior leakage, and you know that the leak has been fixed, you might consider putting a new face on the floor of the cabinet. Stained, warped, and rotted floors of sink cabinets leave a bad impression, even if there is no current leakage.

Bathtub and Shower Area

A tub that is well sealed against moisture will stand up well against all the showers, baths, and even the water fights of little ones. But small voids that allow water penetration can cause big problems. Many new tubs today are one-piece units, with no joints that need to be caulked or cleaned. Older units will have a ceramic tile, fiberglass, or even plastic finish on the walls surrounding the tub. You will want to check the area where the surround meets the tub to be sure there are no voids. If the caulk is dirty, messy, or moldy, it may be worthwhile to pull out the old caulk and put a fresh clean application on now. In addition, be sure to check the grout between the tiles, and fill any voids that you might find. It is always a pleasure for an inspector to find a nicely maintained bath area.

Be sure to check the drain plug and the shower diverter for proper functioning. If your bathroom has a stall shower, look it over to see if it needs repairs or caulking, also. Check the area where the tub or shower meets the floor for unattended leaks, which can cause big problems for you. When water penetrates into floors over time, they can become soft and rotted, sometimes damaging the framing members as well.

If your bathroom has a whirlpool or Jacuzzi, it is a good idea to give it a test run, especially if you have not used it in a while. Sometimes the joints and hoses can dry out and crack when not used regularly, causing unexpected leaks. You don't want to find out at the inspection that your Jacuzzi needs repair. On one inspection, I discovered a dry-rotted pipe by the dripping ceiling above a beautiful wood dining-room table. Luckily, the leak was caught before irreversible damage was caused, but it almost ended the sale right then and there.

Vent Fan

Check the vent fan in the bathroom, making sure it works properly, is not overly noisy, and is clean. If necessary, vacuum it out and use a spray lubricant if the fan is slow or noisy. As we have already discussed in the section on attics, you know to check that the fan vents to the outside and not into the attic.

Wiring

Most bathrooms today are equipped with a GFCI plug, protecting you and your loved ones from power surges and electrocution. If your bathroom has this safety feature, it is a good idea to push the test button and reset it. Of course, if it is not working properly, consult with an electrician.

Your bathroom should now be ready for a good showing in the inspection.

Bedrooms and Living Spaces

The bedrooms and living areas of your home—the kitchen, family room, living room, dining area—often make the strongest impression on your potential buyer, as he will be picturing himself in his daily routine in your home. You want to be sure that he is envisioning a pleasant picture!

Kitchen

The kitchen is a room that can yield big rewards, as it's the room used most by all buyers. Have you ever noticed that at social gatherings people just seem to congregate in and around the kitchen? It serves as the hub of a home, so you want to be sure it is as inviting, and as serviceable, as possible.

Cabinets, Countertops, and Appliances

Clean the cabinets, adjust the hardware and hinges, and check the drawers for smooth operation. Remove clutter from the counters, making it look as spacious as possible. Check the operation of all your appliances—making sure each burner element of the stove works, including the broiler and oven elements. If you have a ventilator with a filter, be sure to clean it now, and replace the lightbulb if it is not working. How about the dishwasher—does the door open properly or does it fall heavily? This may be an indication that the door springs are in need of adjustment or replacement. Does the dishwasher drain without coming up into the sink? If your kitchen is equipped with a garbage disposal, be sure that it is running properly for the inspection. It may be the time to remove or replace it if it is defective.

All Living Areas

Walls and Ceilings

In each of the interior rooms, take a slow walk around, noticing the finishes on your ceilings and walls. If there are water stains, they indicate a red flag to an inspector, prompting a check for moisture content. If that old roof leak was fixed and the stain is still there, it is best to seal it and repaint for a better presentation. While some minor cracks in ceilings are to be expected, wide cracks and cracks that have caused part of the ceiling to drop down are best repaired, taped, and repainted. You may need to hire a professional to do this if you are unfamiliar with sheetrock repairs.

It also may be time to repaint any rooms that are faded, dulled by smoke, or painted with unique paint colors such as purple or orange. In most cases, a neutral color, such as ivory or light gray, is the best presentation for a typical buyer. Look over the walls closely for any holes that might need filling with compound. This is usually a quick job that you can do yourself with a spackling knife and a small can of compound (both can be found in the paint section of your hardware store). Once the compound dries, lightly sand it, and you are ready for painting.

Carpeting and Flooring

While you may not want to invest in new carpeting if yours is old and stained, it is usually worthwhile to have it cleaned by a professional company. Some of the larger companies offer specials on multiple rooms; check your local paper for advertised specials.

If the floors are wood, a buffing may be all that is needed. This is a job that you can do yourself with a can of buffing wax and a buffing machine. They are usually easy to handle and fairly inexpensive to rent. If the wood floors are worn, scratched, or stained, it may be a good investment to have the floors refinished, which involves sanding the wood and applying several coats of finish to protect it. While this might be an unplanned expense (in the range of several hundred dollars per room), wood floors are very often a selling point in a home. In fact, if old carpet is covering hardwood floors, you may do well by removing the carpet and refinishing the floors. Again, consult with your realtor on the advantages to this.

Look closely at ceramic floors for hairline cracks, loose tiles, and missing or loose grout. The only way to address cracks is to replace the cracked tile, which can be done only if you have extra tiles. If you do not have matching tiles, the cracks will have to remain, but you can resecure loose tiles with mastic cement (available at hardware stores in the floor section), and remove loose grout and refill with new, clean grout.

Windows

Be sure to check the windows in each room, making sure they open and close easily, and that the hardware is intact and works properly. Applying a lubricant to the hardware, or silicone to sticky units, will improve the inspection process. Although cleaning the glass may seem burdensome, it will enhance the view, and is an inexpensive task that gives a lasting impression. If the windows are casement (windows that swing out), be sure that all the handles are properly installed and work well. Quite often, homes with central air conditioning have windows that are seldom used, and therefore screens are not installed, and the windows become stuck in place. If you have this situation, it is advisable to install the screens and work on loosening up window sashes as needed. Check all of the sash frames to be sure that a clear finish, stain, or paint has been applied. This will protect the wood from water staining and fading from sunlight. If your windows have been stained from condensation, it may be prudent to restain or paint them to avoid buyer concern.

Doors

Interior doors are important, as they can indicate settling of the building. Many sales have gone bad as a result of uneven door closure. You should go from room to room, opening and closing each door, while noting the gaps between the door and frame. They should be fairly even all the way around, with door stops so they work properly. If any of the units are unusually bad, it may be worthwhile to consult with a carpenter to adjust them, or in some cases, rehang the unit.

Sometimes, uneven closing of doors is caused by movement in a home. This can be a structural concern, and can become a major issue in the sale of your home. If you have trimmed your doors to fit, and found after a period of a few months that they begin to stick or won't close, this is a sign of continued movement. It is time to consult with a structural engineer to determine the cause of movement. While this may be a costly endeavor (many engineers charge several hundred dollars per hour), you may prevent irreparable damage to your home. Once the cause of the movement is addressed, the doors can be rehung to close properly.

If any part of the door unit is damaged, repair or replacement should be done. The hardware should be in good condition; a new lockset will cost $20 or so, and may be well worth this small investment. Have a carpenter adjust any bifold doors (the folding doors on closets) in your home, as it is very common to see them hanging loose or off the tracks at inspections.

Stairs

Stairs are a safety issue as they cause the most injuries in a home. You should tighten any loose railings or handrails and install additional spindles to close in overly wide spaces between them. This will serve to protect small children and pets from falling through or getting stuck. Loose or cracked treads, risers, or stringers should be replaced. Any unusual stair safety condition should be improved or altered to provide the safest design possible.

Wiring

The outlets or switches should have cover plates installed. Check the light fixtures in all rooms to make sure that necessary bulbs are replaced. Loose or missing fixtures should be repaired as needed.

Prepare the interior of the home for the inspection by cleaning out clutter from the rooms, making it easy for the inspector to access areas such as the load center and attic access. Remove stored cars from the garage and empty wastebaskets, as they can harbor smells. Consider leaving a note for the inspector regarding anything that may be helpful, such as the location of garage door openers, hidden switches, locations of supplementary load centers (panel boxes), multiple water heaters, or hidden reset buttons. This type of information will be highly valued by the inspector and might make for a more positive attitude even when a defect is discovered.

Finally, on the day of your inspection, pay attention to the weather. If adverse weather is forecast (such as snow), make sure the walk is shoveled, the driveway plowed, and icy areas sanded. If it is hot, use your air conditioner or fans to improve the environment. Keep your thermostat set to a comfortable temperature on cold days, which will make your buyer feel comfortable about this decision. The buyer, inspectors, and agents will be in the home for quite some time, often several hours, and you want them to leave with a positive feeling about the house. Some sellers will provide tea or coffee (hot or iced, depending on the weather) for the agents and buyers in the hopes of making the whole process less stressful.

While you may choose to take all of these suggestions, or just prioritize and focus on those that you feel are most important, any of these improvements will increase your chances of successfully selling your home for the best price in your area.

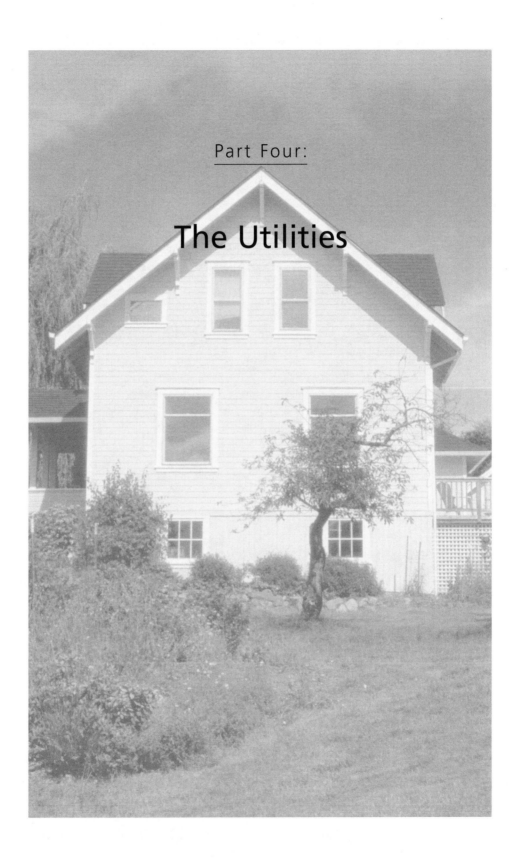

Part Four:

The Utilities

Heating

Homes are heated by a variety of heating systems, utilizing a variety of fuel sources. Your heating system may be a boiler, where water is heated and circulated through piping that radiates the heat into the home. With this system, you may also have the old-fashioned radiator system, usually with one radiator in each room that delivers the heat. Old-fashioned as they may look, they are quite effective when in good running condition. Your heat may be supplied by a furnace that heats the air and circulates it through the ductwork with registers in each room. In some southern climates, you may have one central unit that serves the whole house, which should provide enough heat in these warmer climates. Of course, there is always electric heat, either baseboard or radiant heat. Electric baseboard heat can be advantageous because each room generally has a thermostat and can be zoned according to the living style of each homeowner. Radiant heat, whether floor or ceiling, is a slower delivery system and also has pros and cons. Radiant heat in the floor is wonderful in the wintertime, as your floors will always be nice and warm. The downside is if repairs are needed, the floor has to be pulled up. This can be expensive if you have to remove ceramic tile or hardwood floors. Radiant ceiling heat eliminates the need for baseboard heaters around the perimeter of a room (allowing easier furniture placement), but can cause cracking in the ceilings, and is also difficult to repair if it is defective. No matter what type of heat you have, you want to make sure that it provides an adequate amount of heat for the coldest days in your climate.

Examining Your Heating Unit

Heating systems generally use oil, propane, or natural gas, or electricity as a fuel source. Like all mechanical things, your heating system can deteriorate with age and become more prone to breakdowns. With this in mind, if your unit is an older one, it is advantageous to have accurate records of the service history. If the system is more than twenty-five years old, most inspectors will note that it is at the end of its life expectancy, warning the buyer to anticipate replacement soon. Even if the unit is functioning well, this will be considered a negative factor. It is common knowledge that the newer units are highly efficient, saving money on operating costs and service calls. This is important to keep in mind if you are considering replacing your heating system before the house is listed. You may want to consult with your realtor first.

Preparing the System for Inspection

The inspector will operate the system, so make it easy for him: Be sure to have any shut-off switches turned on; have the service tags readily available to be viewed; and move storage and debris away from the unit. If the unit hasn't been serviced recently, have it cleaned and tuned by a heating technician prior to listing your home. A furnace, being a warm-air system, has a filter that should be changed at least once during the season. It will deliver the heat through ductwork that should be examined for any voids or rusted areas. If it is a boiler, which is a water system (hydronic), look for obvious leaks. Some systems have a flue pipe that vents the exhaust to the exterior. This should be examined for any obvious rusted or separated areas. Many systems have more than one zone, which means you would have two or more thermostats in your house. Be sure to operate all the thermostats and verify that heat is getting to all the zones. Of course, if any of the thermostats are broken or damaged, now is the time to repair them. If your home is to be inspected in the cold weather, turn the heat up prior to the inspection and leave it at a comfortable temperature. While it may cost you a few extra dollars, it will make your buyer more comfortable about the adequacy of the heat.

Checking the Interior Components

You'll want to check the interior heating components also, making sure the baseboard covers are in their proper place. If any are missing, a heating supply house or home center may have replacement panels. Sometimes, old rusty covers can be lightly sanded and repainted for a much nicer presentation. Pay special attention to the radiator cover in the bathrooms, as very often these are most likely to be the ones that rust. Older cast-iron radiators also should be painted if they need it, but consult with your local paint store for the best paint to use on this surface. There are paints that are designed for surfaces that get hot, so you don't have the paint smell each time you turn the unit on.

Heating Units Insulated with Asbestos

One of the things inspectors don't like to find is the presence of asbestos in a home. Older heating systems were often insulated with asbestos, which is a terrific insulating material. Unfortunately, as it deteriorates, it becomes "friable" (or crumbly), and is considered a hazardous material. If you suspect asbestos, there are companies that can verify this through testing. While some products made of asbestos are easily identifiable (see p. 88), there are others that can only be determined through testing. Asbestos abatement companies are in the business of asbestos removal, and they will usually provide a cost estimate for removal. Anytime removal of environmentally hazardous materials is involved, the cost can be in the thousands, as special precautions are needed and the materials have to be transported to specific facilities that accept these materials. If your home does have the presence of asbestos, this can be a major concern that might terminate the sale, so it is best to do some research ahead of time and avoid having your sale fall apart. Refer to the chapter on environmental hazards for more information.

Underground Fuel Tanks

Another area of concern for buyers is the presence of underground fuel tanks, even if they are not currently being used. As recently as twenty years ago, it was common practice to put a metal fuel storage tank in the ground, in order to hide this eyesore, or to avoid taking up valuable space in a small basement. While it may have seemed like a fine idea at first, many tanks became rusty and leaked oil into the ground, creating an environmental disaster. Soils, ponds, and wells have been contaminated with oil, which takes years to dissipate. Today, if you have evidence of a leaky underground oil storage tank, the DEP in many states will hold you responsible for the cleanup, which involves removing all the contaminated soil surrounding the tank.

If you know of any abandoned or active underground tanks, it would be best to deal with them prior to the sale. While the cost of tank removal may be several hundred dollars, it could prevent an eventual major cleanup cost of thousands of dollars, and possibly more than ten thousand dollars if the tank were to leak. It is very likely that your sale will be contingent upon your having the tank removed, so you should make this your first priority before listing your house. Once you have the tank removed by a reputable company, be sure to keep all documentation, as this will be important to pass on to the buyer. Inspectors will often notice the evidence of an underground tank even after it has been removed, and you want to show documentation that it was removed with no environmental spill. And if you smell oil or gas, by all means call a service company immediately.

Another condition to note is if any of the fuel lines are installed through concrete. Most inspectors will recommend that lines going underground (either through the concrete or dirt) should be installed in a conduit to prevent deterioration and leaking. If you

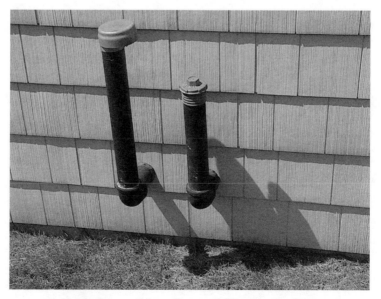

Check the condition of your oil fill and vent pipes.
They may need to be repaired if they are rusted.

have this condition, it might save you trouble if you have your heating technician re-work the lines when the unit is serviced. You might also consider painting the fill and vent pipes (on oil systems) on the outside, particularly if they are rusted. Keep in mind that these small tasks are well worth it if they serve to prevent oil from seeping into the ground, and possibly into a water supply.

Electric Heating Units

Electric heat units should each be tested, including the individual wall units often found in bathrooms, to be sure they are operational on the day of the inspection. Take a look inside them to see if they need cleaning or vacuuming.

Keeping Units in Working Order

Finally, walk around the interior rooms. Vacuum out heating registers where needed, and move items away from the heat source so nothing gets burned during the testing. If the registers are worn they can be replaced or spray-painted for a better appearance. You should replace loose or broken covers. Sometimes older radiators have drips or leaks evident at the valves, in which case a plumber should be consulted. Prior to the inspection, make sure the burner switch is turned on, as they are often turned off in the summer months.

Plumbing

As the current owner of the home, you probably feel comfortable that you have no leaky pipes or problematic plumbing, but we have surprised more than a few home-owners with undetected leaks and other issues. Don't wait for the home inspector to find them. Let's do a regular maintenance check of your plumbing now.

In the Kitchen

We can start in the kitchen, by turning on the kitchen faucet and swinging the arm back and forth. You want to look for water coming out of the faucet at the base, or at the handles. Water pooling around the sink can often spill back onto the counter, eventually causing damage under the Formica or in the walls. Does the faucet drip when you turn it off, or do you have to tighten it hard to get it to stop? An inexpensive washer may take care of the problem. While the water is running, check under the sink with a flashlight for any drips or leaks. If you know a leak has occurred, and you've given it a temporary fix, now is the time to have it repaired properly. While you are under there, take a peek at the feed lines for any drips also. Finally, look at the floor of the cabinet for evidence of prior drips.

In the Bathrooms

Do the same in each of the bathrooms, checking the sinks for obvious issues. When checking the bathroom sinks, make sure that the drain mechanism is working properly and adjust it if necessary. It is a good idea to fill the bathroom sink until it drains into the overflow outlet, and then open the drain. In this way, if there is a previously undetected leak, the pressure will surely allow you to see it. The tub deserves special attention, as this is where we can find a tremendous amount of damage.

First, you want to make sure your valves are in good working order, and the diverter works properly to change the flow of water from the faucet to the showerhead. Of course, you want to be sure that the area where the valves and faucet go through the surround are watertight, so as to prevent water penetration behind the surround. Close the drain and run a little water in the tub. Check it in a while to see if the water is still there. While many people can overlook a sink that does not hold water, a bathtub is a different story, particularly if your buyer has small children. Be sure to flush the toilets, making sure they stop running as designed. Look at the feed line coming out from the wall, or up from the floor, checking for leaks or unusual corrosion. Many times the bottom of the sink cabinet has evidence of leakage or damage from past leaks. I have seen many buyers turn away from a deal just by looking into a cabinet that has black mold along with a damaged cabinet floor. If this is the case, proper repair procedures should be done as necessary.

Water Filters

If the home has a water sediment filter, this should definitely be changed regularly, depending upon the amount of sediment in your water. Old filters can harbor bacteria and result in a poor water test, which can often break a deal. If the home has a well, you want to make sure that it is properly sealed or capped. If the cover is less than ideal, now would be the time to improve it. Shallow wells should have a heavy concrete top that fits over the entire opening of the well; you can check with a local concrete company for precast well covers. Your yellow-pages directory can help, under the heading "Concrete—precast products." A drilled well can often be seen sticking out of the ground with a metal cap on it. If this cap is not securely fastened, check with a well-drilling contractor for a replacement cap.

Consider having the water tested for bacteria, and if present, the well should be chlorinated. A water profile will determine your pH level, as well as levels of other components such as iron, manganese, etc. You can also purchase test kits that will allow you to pretest for specific results. Keep in mind that very few wells come out with a perfect profile. Coliform bacteria are more common than most people realize, and it is valuable to know if your well needs treatment. If E. coli bacteria are present, it can be an indication of fecal or septic contamination. Of course, this is a serious issue and should be addressed immediately for your own family's safety.

Supply Lines and Drainpipes

In the basement of your home, look at your supply lines and drainpipes, noting any active leaks, corrosion, or need for additional supports. Drainpipes should gradually pitch down to the main clean-out. We often come across drainpipes that are leaking, so it is a good idea to run all the water in the home and examine drainpipes with a bright flashlight. Your drainpipes are the larger-diameter pipes, while your feed lines (which deliver the water to the home) are smaller in diameter. Have any leaks you find repaired by your plumber.

From the outside, check if your home has a vent pipe extending from the roof. A vent pipe allows your pipes to drain properly without slowing down or causing undue drain noise. If you do not have a vent pipe, a plumber should be consulted. Supply piping (domestic hot and cold lines) should be looked over also. Sometimes minor leaks can be found at the valves or along the length tubing, whether copper or plastic, and of course, they should be repaired.

In the Crawl Space

If the home has a crawl area and you don't want to crawl all around in there, have someone flush toilets, and run the showers and sinks while you listen for leaking water (this procedure was also addressed on page 48. In this way, you can pinpoint any areas that might need your attention.

Water Heater

Examine your water heater, looking for any signs of deterioration or leaks. Unfortunately, if the unit is leaking, it may need to be replaced, but it is better to address it now rather than have it discovered at an inspection. The cost of a standard electric unit and installation should be around $450 to $650, with oil or gas units costing slightly more. You will want to note any rust spots or corrosion that might warn of an impending problem. Your water heater should be fitted with a relief valve, which is designed to release if the water gets overheated. This is a precautionary device to keep the unit from exploding, but the valve should have a pipe running down the side and ending about six to eight inches from the floor. If hot steam is released, it would be less likely to harm anyone standing close by the unit, particularly young children. Many home centers now have premade discharge tubes that can be easily installed with water pipe pliers or a wrench. If you have noticed any problems with insufficient hot water, you might want to have the water heater unit checked. The problem may simply be a burned-out electrical element. If the unit is gas or oil, look at the flue pipe and have it repaired if any holes are evident. Be sure to move stored items away from the water heater, making it easier for the inspector to access.

Expansion Tank

If the home has a well, look at the expansion tank that is usually located near the main valve. Newer-type tanks have a bladder in them, so the tank should have a hollow sound when tapped with a screwdriver. If the tank has any obvious leaks, a replacement may be needed, and you should consult with a plumber. If you notice condensation on the exterior, don't be concerned as this is normal.

Water Pressure

How is your water pressure? Is there a substantial drop when two or more fixtures are running? A slight drop in pressure is common. However, if you note obvious pressure problems, have a plumber evaluate the situation. And, if there is a water treatment system, have it serviced or change filters if needed. Some systems have a brine tank that requires salts to be added on a regular basis in order to soften the water. If this is the case, check to see that the salt levels are adequate. Also, have any information on the water treatment system available for your buyer, such as your service contact information, service schedule, operating instructions, and any other pertinent information. It is also a good idea to provide information on the reason behind the water treatment system. Is it taking out minerals, such as rust or manganese? Or is it adding something, such as salts to treat the water? These are questions that any buyer will want to have answered.

Outside Faucets

Walk around the exterior of your home and check the operation of the outside hose bibs or faucets. If they are not frost-free hose bibs, be sure they are turned off and drained in winter climates, as they can freeze, and possibly burst. Installing frost-free hose bibs is a convenience that you will likely appreciate when the cold winter months arrive.

You can now feel comfortable with the typical issues regarding the plumbing in your home.

Electrical

Although I recommend that you retain the services of a professional electrician or inspector to thoroughly assess the condition of your electrical system, there are some things that you can visually note to determine if this part of your home needs immediate attention or not. As we pointed out in the outdoors section of this book, you want to make sure that the entry wire coming from the weatherhead (see picture) to your meter box is in good shape. If it is frayed, hanging loose, or does not seem to be in good condition, you definitely want to correct this prior to the sale. If your home has underground utilities, most of your service wire will not be exposed. Look at your meter socket; check the box for rust or deterioration. An electrician can work together with the electric company to get the entry wire and meter box in proper order.

It is important that your weatherhead, entry wire, and meter box are all in working order. This is something that should be high on your list of priorities.

Load Center or Panel Box

From the interior of the house, you want to locate the load center, or panel box. It could be located almost anywhere, but is commonly found in the basement, or in a closet. If you have a difficult time locating it, find the entry location of the main feed wire, and then look in that area on the inside. The first thing you need to do is to clear out the area around it for easy access. Most homes today have breaker-type load centers, which will allow a switch to trip off if there is an overload on the circuit. If your load center is the old fuse-style panel, it can present a problem. Although these worked well for many years, the danger arises when people install 30-amp fuses where only a 15-amp fuse should be. This could allow more electricity to pass through, possibly heating up the circuit and wires and eventually causing a fire. Many insurance companies today will not accept fuse panels, citing them as a fire hazard. You might want to consult with an electrician on the cost to update the panel box at this time.

An old fuse panel like this one should be removed and
replaced with an updated load center.

As you look at your panel box, check the sides, top, and bottom to see if there are any openings. These openings are an invitation to mice and insects, which can cause chaos in your home. Rodents seem to love chewing on the plastic wire covering—we have found our fair share of fried surprises in a load center. You can purchase small inserts from your local hardware store (check the electrical section) to install in the box that will close up some of the small round openings that you might find there. Also, be sure that the cover is on and securely attached. When a cover is missing, it puts anyone getting near it at great risk. On one of my recent inspections, an open load center was discovered deep inside a kitchen cabinet. Anyone reaching in the cabinet in search of something could have easily connected with unprotected wires and been electrocuted—an accident waiting to happen! In other sections of this book, we addressed the importance of fixing open junction boxes, open splices, loose or damaged light fixtures, and broken outlets.

Outlets

Most new homes today have Ground Fault Circuit Interrupters (or GFCI) outlets installed in the kitchen, bathrooms, and exterior outlets, which are designed to trip when a surge or disruption of electricity is caused, thereby providing safety to the people using them. While older homes may not have these, it is an investment worth considering. Most electricians can do this for you without much difficulty. These outlets are generally around $20 each, plus the cost of installation by your electrician. If you do have GFCI outlets, push and reset the test buttons to be sure that they are working correctly.

Is Your Wiring Safe?

The type of wiring you use can be an important consideration. Newer homes have Romex wiring, which has the white plastic covering. Some homes have BX—the armored steel wiring—which is usually fine, but be sure to examine it for any rusted areas. Some older homes have fabric-covered wiring, which should be examined carefully for defects, or knob and tube wiring which should be upgraded, especially the areas tied into Romex or BX.

This BX cable is improperly spliced and taped,
creating a safety and fire hazard.

Older wiring that is frayed or taped, and rusty BX wire, can present problems in your sale. These conditions should be addressed by an electrician. A buyer may not be able to secure a mortgage if some of the older types of wiring are in place, especially if knob and tube wires are present. Upgrading the wiring may eliminate serious issues with the inspection process, avoiding termination of the contract and certainly adding value to your home.

Both exterior and interior light fixtures should be examined for obvious defects. Check to see if they are loose, hanging, or damaged. Some of them may simply be outdated and upgrading them may give a better presentation. I have seen some fairly nice-looking fixtures priced as low as $20 in home centers. The relatively low cost of replacing a few may be well worth the investment.

Smoke Detectors

Finally, check your smoke detectors, making sure they are properly installed with new batteries and are working correctly. Of course, you could fill a room with smoke to see if they are working correctly, but they also have a test button to make it easy on you. Pressing the test button should make the unit emit a loud piercing sound that should stop within five seconds. If they do not stop on their own, it may be an indication that the unit is defective. To stop the alarm, you can remove the battery and replace it, or if it is a hardwired unit (run by electricity), you will have to call an electrician to have it replaced.

There are other defects, such as double-tap wiring, ungrounded outlets, and reversed polarity outlets that could be uncovered in an inspection. However, these conditions require the use of testing equipment that you may not have readily available. If you are concerned about other issues, it would be advisable to contact an electrician.

Part Five:

Special Considerations

Environmental Hazards

Today's home buyers are very savvy, and are concerned about many health hazards, including:

- radon in air and water;
- water quality and contamination;
- lead paint;
- asbestos;
- soil contamination;
- mold; and
- air quality.

While many sales will not be contingent upon testing for all of these situations, the results of the home inspection may warrant further testing in one or more of the areas. The most common additional tests requested today are for radon in the air, and water potability. This section will provide a brief overview of the tests and the reasoning behind them.

Testing for Radon in Air

Radon is a radioactive gas occurring in nature, which results from the decay of uranium. Radon can be found in high concentrations in soils and rocks containing uranium. It is invisible, tasteless, and odorless, so would go undetected without the use of specialized testing. The U.S. Surgeon General, Dr. Richard Carmona, noted that 20,000 Americans die each year from radon-related lung cancer, and released the National Health Advisory on Radon on January 13, 2005. This advisory restated the danger of breathing air with high levels of radon for prolonged periods. His press release can be found on the U.S. Department of Health and Human Services Web site, http://www.surgeongeneral.gov/pressreleases/sg01132005.html.

As a result of this advisory, the EPA is issuing an annual reminder to Americans to test for radon gas in their homes. For more information on radon gas, you can visit their Web site (http://www.epa.gov/radon/) or call 1–800–767–7236. Most home buyers today will have their home tested for radon in the air as a part of the purchase agreement. There are a variety of testing methods, but most home inspectors will utilize a short-term test for timely results. If the test results are higher than the recommended level, there are mitigation systems that can be installed, keeping the radon at an acceptable level. The cost of a system depends, of course, on many variables, but can be between $1,000 and $1,500. As a homeowner, you can purchase kits from hardware and home improvement stores, but the canisters provided in these kits often must be mailed out to a laboratory. If you need fairly quick results, it may be prudent to call a home inspector or a local laboratory to do the testing for you. Check your yellow-pages directory under "Radon."

Make Your Mind Up About Selling Your Home

Many sellers become possessive of their homes, even though they are the ones who decided to sell them. In one case, a woman was upset that the buyer had contracted to have a radon test done. The seller insisted that if she did not want the canisters in her house, it was her prerogative to refuse the test. Though an issue of it was not made at the time of the inspection, the next day the realtor called and informed us that the woman had agreed to allow the test to be performed. She quickly realized that though it was her prerogative to refuse the test, it was also the prerogative of the buyer to refuse to buy the house without the test being performed.

Testing for Radon in Water

Testing for radon in water is less common, often done when test results are high for radon in the air, as radon in well water can contribute to the indoor air levels of radon gas. Currently, the EPA has no requirements regarding radon in water. Studies are still being conducted, and recommendations discussed, but a recommendation under consideration is to install a reduction system if the level is above 4,000 picocuries per liter. Radon in the air presents a greater risk of lung cancer than radon in drinking water, so the mitigation levels are vastly different. For more information on radon in drinking water, visit the EPA Web site at http://www.epa.gov/safewater/radon.html.

It is important to note that the radon levels in your air and water can fluctuate, depending on several factors. Testing of radon in the air requires a closed house, and is best done if the home has been closed for at least twenty-four hours prior to initiating the test. Winter testing for radon usually results in higher readings, but testing over several weeks is the most accurate, as it will give an average result over time. This is generally not reasonable for a sales contract, which is why most radon tests are conducted over a two- to seven-day period.

Water Quality Testing

The quality of the water is always of great concern to home buyers. If your home has city water, it is not usually common to have the water tested by the buyer, as it is regularly tested by the supplier (the utility company or the municipality). When your home is served by a private or shared well, it is likely that the water will be tested. While some people believe that they would know if there was a problem with the water, we have surprised many sellers with the test results revealing contamination of their water with bacteria. It is recommended that you have a water sample tested prior to the sale, so as to avoid these unwanted surprises that might stop the sale. A basic water profile will tell you if you have the presence of either coliform or E. coli bacteria. It will also give you the levels of iron, manganese, sodium, and pH in your water. If there are any problems, you can consult with a water treatment company for recommendations.

"Love that Dirty Water?"

I recall one case where the seller was a gentleman who greeted us by saying there was no need to inspect his house as it was so well maintained. When drawing the water in the same home, the man commented that there was no need to test it, since he had been drinking that water for years. Needless to say, he was quite surprised when the lab test came back positive for fecal bacteria. The seller finally had to drill a new well in order to preserve the sale.

At the very least, if your water does have bacteria, you will want to address that issue prior to listing your home. Checking the condition of the well prior to the inspection is a good idea. Seal any obvious openings that might allow a mouse to get into the well, and make sure the well cap is secure to prevent children from falling into it. Also, be sure that your dog is not tied anywhere near your well, and keep hazardous materials such as old batteries, stored oil, or old antifreeze away from your well. Any contamination by hazardous waste will render a well useless for some time, and could potentially cost you thousands of dollars. Lead in water may also be a concern, as old houses may contain some lead piping or lead in the solder that was used prior to 1978. Your water can be tested for lead content if that is a concern.

Underground Fuel Tanks

Another cause for concern is underground storage tanks, most commonly used for the storage of oil to fuel the heating system. State policy concerning legalities of commercial or residential tanks may vary, but it is my opinion that removing the tank may be the best way to avoid problems. The unexpected discovery of an underground oil tank can scare many buyers off, even if you are willing to pay to have it removed. The cost for tank removal can vary, depending on landscaping, accessibility, depth of the tank, and the ultimate condition of the tank. It is best to hire a company that specializes in tank removal, as you do not want to cause problems that did not already exist. When an oil tank is removed, it is critical that it be removed intact so no oil spills into the soil or water supply. If this happens, you will be faced with a cleanup that can cost thousands of dollars, as it will likely involve soil removal and replacement, as well as long-term testing. Remember to keep your documentation on the successful tank removal so no question arises about the procedure. This documentation should be passed on to the new owner for future reference.

It is wise to disclose as much information about any underground fuel tanks to your buyer as possible. Here is evidence that an underground fuel tank exists on this property.

Lead

There is no question that lead in paint can cause problems, and the fact remains that most homes built before the 1970s are likely to contain lead paint. There are two pertinent warnings that are worthwhile reading from the Consumer Protection Bureau regarding lead in paint:

1. *What You Should Know About Lead-Based Paint in Your Home: Safety Alert—CPSC Document #5054* is available at www.cpsc.gov/CPSCPUB/PUBS/5054.html.

2. *CPSC Warns About Hazards of "Do It Yourself" Removal of Lead-Based Paint: Safety Alert—CPSC Document #5055* is available at www.cpsc.gov/CPSCPUB/PUBS/5055.html.

Many homes have been painted several times, so if the paint does not display any chipping, peeling, or deterioration, it may be okay. On the other hand, when the exterior of an older home has been scraped over the years, the paint chips can permeate into the soil, contaminating it. Children playing in this area can be poisoned by this contaminated soil. Testing for lead content can be accomplished through the use of an XRF paint analyzer, which is actually a portable X-ray gun that will determine the presence of lead through all the layers of paint and give a surface-by-surface report on the results. Only certified operators can perform this testing method. Check your yellow-pages directory under "Lead Testing" for companies that specialize in this technique.

Keep in mind that lead-based paint that is in good condition and not likely to chip, cause dust, or be chewed on by a child is not considered a hazard. If you do have chipping, flaking paint that is lead-based, it is important to hire a reputable company for removal (which includes scraping and containment of all the paint chips and dust), or be familiar with the proper precautions in removing lead-based paint. In the past, many homeowners have scraped away paint from their homes, allowing the dust and chips to permeate in the ground around the home. Soil and water contamination can occur from this careless practice, and may ultimately poison the occupants. You can also get more information regarding the hazards of lead in paint, dust, and soil at http://www.epa.gov/lead/index.html.

Federal law requires that a disclosure be issued to buyers if there is knowledge of lead-based paint. It is recommended that you do your research on lead-based paint prior to listing your home.

Mold

Another recent concern of buyers is the indoor air quality of the home, particularly regarding the presence of mold. Studies show that some people are allergic to certain mold spores, and that their presence can make the occupants ill. There are many ways to test for mold, but keep in mind that the levels vary from day to day, depending on weather, moisture concerns, and other factors. As the homeowner, you can do some things to prevent moisture problems and the possibility of mold growth. Bathroom fans should be operational and ducted to the exterior of the home. Vents in crawl spaces and attics should be adequate in size and opened during warm weather. Gutters should be kept clean and the drains should extend away from the home. Basement or crawl space leakage problems should be addressed or improved as quickly as possible. Windows and doors should be caulked and roof leaks promptly repaired. Finished surfaces that have water stains from past leakage or evidence of prior black mold should be cleaned, sealed, and repainted before a showing. If necessary, replace sections of interior surfaces that are damaged from moisture. Keep in

Where would you most likely find asbestos in your home?
One place that may have it is your basement. Asbestos was often
used to wrap heat pipes connected to the furnace.

mind that if you are cleaning areas with black mold, it is recommended that you wear protective covering, such as protective breathing apparatus and safety goggles, and if you are highly allergic, hire a professional to do the job.

Asbestos

The discovery of asbestos can easily cause a buyer to walk away from a contract, particularly if the asbestos is in poor shape. Asbestos is a fibrous material used extensively in many building products in homes built prior to 1975. Thousands of building products—so many that it is impossible to identify most of them—had some component of asbestos in them. The two most common usages identified today are asbestos shingles on the exterior of a home (the siding), and asbestos wrapping on heat pipes in basements. Researchers have identified three diseases associated with the inhalation of asbestos fibers: asbestosis, lung cancer, and mesothelioma of the pleura, all of which are debilitating. (You can find more information on asbestos exposure at http://www.atsdr.cdc.gov/asbestos/asbestos_effects.html.)

Asbestos was once widely used due to its insulative qualities and strength, but today we know it is a hazardous material, particularly if it is deteriorated or friable, which means that the asbestos can be crushed into a powder by hand and can easily become airborne—this is not something that you want to test, though! The identification of products containing asbestos in your home will often raise a red flag and may cause problems with the contract. The only sure way to determine the presence of asbestos is through a lab test, but if you are concerned that your home may have an asbestos component, it is advisable to contact an asbestos abatement company. They will come out and advise you on removal and costs—which can vary, depending on the product and amount of material—but can cost up to thousands of dollars to remove. On the other hand, if you have a floor covered with asbestos tiles (usually 9-by-9-inch tiles), the company may recommend covering it with subflooring and laying a new finished floor over it. In some cases, containment of a hazardous material is an acceptable method. At the very least, if you are aware of asbestos in your home, you must disclose it to the buyer.

These environmental concerns can be very important in the final sale of your home, so should be discussed with your realtor. Certainly, we feel it is better to know all the hazards, particularly for the health and safety of all occupants of the home.

The Condominium

Inspections of condominiums are becoming more common today, as there are still many issues that can adversely affect the value of a unit. There are many components of a condominium that are the financial responsibility of the homeowners association, and are not inspected in a typical condo inspection. When inspecting a condo, one of my first recommendations to the buyer is to obtain a copy of the condominium documents, as they usually outline the responsibilities of the owners, the association, and rules and regulations within the complex. As the seller, you may want to have your set available for your agent to review. Check with the association about securing a current copy for your buyer, usually after the contract is signed. Although the exterior is commonly the responsibility of the association, as the inspector, I will still look at it to get a feel for the level of maintenance of the association. I will share whatever information I've gathered with the buyer so that questions directed to the association can be asked about future repair schedules or possible assessments. Many exterior repairs are the responsibility of the condo association, but the value of each condo is reflective of the care and maintenance taken by the association.

The mechanical systems, such as furnaces, air conditioners, and water heaters, are most often the responsibility of the unit owner, so you can refer to the appropriate sections in this book regarding those things. Some associations may require that the water heater be replaced every ten years, so as to protect other owners from damage due to a leaking unit. In some cases the heating system may be shared "in common," in which case it would be the responsibility of association. The appearance and condition of your unit's interior spaces should be your responsibility, so follow the same guidelines listed in Part 2, The Indoors. Windows and doors can be "gray" areas, as each association may handle these features differently. If they are the responsibility of the owner, there may be restrictions or rules governing the type, color, or even manufacturer when replacing the units. All of this information should be in the condominium documents, and we recommend that you retain the services of your attorney to review them for your protection.

"Deal Breakers"— The Most Common Mistakes Sellers Make

As a home inspector, I have noticed that buyers today are much more savvy, educated, and demanding—often utilizing findings from the home inspection to further negotiate the price of the home. When you make every effort to prepare your home before the inspection, you can avoid additional negotiations or the potential loss of the sale.

Don't Let Things Get out of Hand

Most home buyers will expect, even hope, that the inspector will find a few problems. However, as the list grows longer, the buyer begins to get anxious. You, the seller, may have lived for years not knowing or caring about the issues, such as wood rot, that have been discovered at the inspection. It is a big mistake to let a preventable problem with your home get out of hand. Wood rot, for example, is usually caused when unprotected wood is exposed to moisture for a prolonged period of time. Homes in humid regions can begin to show rot in as early as seven years from the time they were built. If the inspector points out several areas of wood rot, the buyer's mind starts to visualize the worst-case scenario, such as interior areas of the structure coming apart. The inspector is also trying to cover his liability, so he will likely explain the possibility of additional, concealed rot. The same can be true about windows and doors. If one window or door doesn't close properly, it is probably not a big deal. However, if several have problems, the buyer's mind starts thinking the worst. If the furnace has not been serviced, has a dirty filter, a rusted flue pipe, and a dirty humidifier, it is likely that the buyer will assume that the furnace has gone some time without service and may envision the need for premature replacement. The idea here is to follow the checklist outlined in this book to reduce the chance of a lost or compromised sale. Under ideal circumstances, regular maintenance of a home, whether on the market or not, is a wise practice.

Don't Become the Cantankerous Seller

Sellers who have lived in a home for most of their lives are still possessive, and can often be defensive about the condition of their house. They insist on staying in the house during the inspection, putting their two cents in whenever they can. They often become easily agitated, resentful of the comments the home inspector makes, and are suspicious in nature. The first thing out of their mouths usually is, "We have lived here for twenty years. You're not going to find anything wrong with this house." Or, "When we bought, there were no home inspectors." They tend to complicate the sale by making mistakes, such as leaving their cars in the garage or driveway, highlighting a potential parking problem for the buyer, and leaving the inspector, buyer, and real estate agents to park in the road. In their minds, everything is fine, from the septic system (which they proudly point out has not been pumped in more than twenty years) to the well water (which has never been tested . . . but they've never gotten sick!). We have seen this type of seller get upset when we run the water for twenty minutes for the water test, or get particularly agitated when termites are discovered. They may also tell the buyer about a neighbor who once had a leaky underground oil tank, or about the time the basement was flooded. Bringing up these old stories from the past may only serve to scare away the buyer. Don't make this mistake.

In most cases, it is best to leave your home during the inspection, letting the real estate agents and inspectors do their jobs. Remember, this home will no longer belong to you—you are hoping that it will become the new home of the buyer. Try to conduct yourself in such a way as to make your buyer feel comfortable about being in the home. If you feel you must stay during the inspection, remember that it's being done for the buyer, so give the inspector and the buyer some privacy while the inspection is being done, particularly while they are discussing the issues.

Attack of the Angry Seller

Most inspectors will show up to an inspection a few minutes early. I remember one occasion when the owner, an elderly woman, told us it was okay to go ahead and get started even though she was about to leave. I proceeded to walk around the outside of the house to take a look at the exterior. Unbeknownst to me, the owner's husband was in the backyard and began cursing at the audacity of our firm to enter someone's property without permission. This made for a less than ideal start, and it only got worse. He proceeded to follow us around everywhere, disputing every one of our findings. While down in the basement, I pointed out evidence of leakage near a toilet to the agents and buyer. Shortly after, the other inspector flushed that very toilet and a rush of water came streaming down. The seller vehemently accused us of breaking his toilet and making false claims about his "perfect" home. By this time, the buyer was so distraught because of the tension that he had to leave before the inspection was completed. Luckily, the sale still went through, although it was tense even at the closing.

Don't Let the Termites Move in with You

These insects cause billions of dollars in damage yearly to wood structures. They actually ingest wood fibers, weakening the wood structures that they attack. These subterranean insects live in the damp ground and tunnel up in mud tubes, allowing them to stay in the dark. They can enter any and all of the wood components of the home. When termites are discovered at an inspection, treatment by an exterminating company is recommended. Professional exterminating is usually done either by chemical treatment to the whole structure or by a baiting method. Always use a professional company with proper documentation, as we have seen cases where a seller got someone who did it as a moonlighting job, and the lack of documentation meant they had to pay to have the property retreated. Consider having your property pre-inspected for termites and take appropriate action if they are discovered. The cost of termite treatment is most often borne by the seller, so you may as well have a termite company do an inspection before you list your home, and proceed with the knowledge that your home is either free of the critters, or has been appropriately treated.

Any damaged wood should be replaced or sistered (adding another member to the side) by a carpenter. Most inspectors will also indicate the possibility of hidden damage, and recommend a consultation with a builder to make the necessary repairs. Remember, the inspector is merely doing a visual inspection and is not allowed to remove wallboard, siding, or any part of the structure.

A "hidden damage clause" in inspection reports is there to protect the inspector, as well as to inform the buyer of potential structural problems. When there is the potential for hidden damage, it can discourage a buyer for good reasons, as it is an unknown regarding the sale. The buyer will likely get the recommendation of a builder, who is also making a judgment on an unknown, so will likely give a "best-case" and "worst-case" estimate. This now puts you, the seller, at a great disadvantage, as the buyer will focus on the higher estimate, and rightfully so.

Don't Let Your Water Send the Deal Down the Drain

Private wells are common in many areas of the country, and so, too, are water problems. If you have city or municipal water, you don't need to worry about water potability, as the supplier is required to do regularly scheduled testing. You could spend hundreds of dollars on water testing for all different things. The most common test for a sales contract is a basic water profile, which covers the basic minerals, sodium, pH level, nitrates/nitrites, and the presence or absence of coliform or E. coli bacteria. It is common to have some problem detected with any water sample. There are many ways to deal with water problems, either through water treatment systems or by removing the source of the problem. Knowing in advance that a problem exists only helps you resolve it without turning your buyer off to the deal.

In other sections of this book, more attention is given to water quality problems and how to solve them. Most inspectors will take a water sample on the day of the home inspection, and a licensed water lab will send the results to the buyer. The presence of bacteria—especially E. coli (or fecal)—in the water can scare a buyer, as it can indicate intrusion from a septic system. Other variations in the water profile can also worry the buyer, so it is best to do your homework first. We recommend that you test your water in advance of listing the home. That way, if a problem surfaces, corrective measures can be taken before they cause a problem.

No Swimming in the Basement, Please

Most basements have experienced water leakage at one time or another, usually during unusual weather conditions. The two main causes of wet basements are a high water table (high groundwater), or surface water and roof runoff entering the basement along the edges of the home. If high groundwater level is evident, be sure to have a properly functioning sump pump. The discharge opening should be well away from the home, preventing the water from flowing back into the basement. Make sure the pump is installed in a professional manner (without a rope being tied to it or an extension cord dangling in the water).

Whether or not you have had water intrusion in your basement, make sure your gutters are clean and pitched properly, and that the downspouts discharge at least five feet from the home. Wet conditions can cause mold and mildew to grow, and this will certainly scare a buyer. If you have done everything possible and wet areas prevail, there are basement de-watering systems that can be installed by contractors, though these can be expensive. Most buyers will become concerned if there are wet conditions present at the time of the inspection, unless this was a condition noted prior to the contract signing.

Squirrels, Bats, and Raccoons Don't Make Good Houseguests

Most people have dealt with controlling some type of vermin over the years. Mice, rats, raccoons, squirrels, skunks, snakes, and bats would all prefer to live in a nice, covered, heated home. But they must all have access in order to get in, so the first thing to do is to discover their entry point, seal them out, and trap/remove the ones that you already have. There are companies or individuals that specialize in trapping or removal of most of these animals, and in some areas, your local environmental agency may direct you to approved trappers for larger animals such as raccoons and skunks. Once you have succeeded in ridding yourself of these pests, you also want to be sure to clean up the evidence left behind. To prevent further intrusion by these animals, we can make a few recommendations:

- chimneys should have rain caps with screens;
- voids in old foundations should be sealed;
- birdseed should be kept away from the exterior of the home;
- garage door seals should be checked;

Squirrels can cause all kinds of damage to your home.
They can knaw on your exterior claboards. They are best dealt with
through your local environmental agency.

Make sure your chimney has a rain cap to
prevent visits from unwanted guests.

- attic spaces should be checked for any open windows or vents that need screening repairs;
- and areas under decks and stairs should be adequately sealed.

While some of this may not have bothered you over the years, many buyers get concerned at the thought of vermin in their new home.

Don't Be Lazy about Your Hazardous Materials

In other sections of this book, we address various environmental concerns in detail, such as underground oil tanks, asbestos, lead, and radon. The point we want to make here is that any one of these issues can bring the sale to a screeching halt. Don't let the discovery of an environmental issue take you and the buyer by surprise. While we are not recommending that you test for all of these components, we do encourage you to follow up if any of these areas have been a concern for you. For instance, if your home is very old, and has some peeling paint around the windowsills, you may want to test for lead paint. If the insulating wrapping around your heating pipes in the basement has been there since before you moved in, you might want to confirm that it is not asbestos. We emphasize that it is important to do your homework if you are aware of hazards; if they can be reduced, or at least disclosed, it will be a selling point. Not all buyers test for all potential hazards; however, a little education and pretesting may eliminate some obstacles.

I Don't Mind the Smell

Contrary to the belief of some, it is not a selling point to admit that you have never had to have your septic system pumped because there never seemed to be any reason to. Just because you are not aware of a problem does not mean that one does not exist. It is best to have your septic system maintained properly, which includes a pump-out every three to five years, more often if there is heavy usage (large family, lots of laundry, etc.). Many homes have private septic systems, and they may have a number of problems that go undetected until they become a big issue. Most buyers today will want to have a full septic inspection, which often includes a pumping out of the tank; a visual inspection of the tank, the baffles (the piping that brings the effluent in and sends the liquids out), and the access cover; as well as an evaluation of the leaching system. Septic failure usually means a substantial cost is likely to be incurred by the buyer or the seller, and this often causes the sale to fall apart. First and foremost, be sure to have your system serviced regularly, as recommended by a septic company, and then consider retaining your service company to do a pre-inspection of your system. This is highly recommended if you have noticed poor flushing, slow drainage, wet areas in your yard, or unusual sewage smells at times. In most cases, it is best to know ahead of time if your septic system is problematic, so you can address the issue on your own terms.

Don't Let the Roof Cave In

There are many conditions in a home that may put undue stress on structural components over the years, and disregarding them will make matters worse and decrease the value of your home. Some issues may need repair or additional support, while others may require the expertise of a structural engineer. Having your home inspected prior to listing it would identify the serious concerns so they can be addressed. There are many carpenters and builders in the field who have a variety of skills and talents. You want to be sure to have a tradesman with the proper qualifications who will properly address the issue, and avoid negative concerns by the inspector. Be sure to check qualifications and references on any carpenter or building company before you hire someone for structural work. If a structural concern, such as a split rafter or notched joist, is addressed properly, using standard practices, it is likely that the inspector will highlight the prior problem and note that an appropriate repair was made, giving everyone a comfort level about the overall maintenance of the home.

If You Don't Know What You're Doing, Don't Do It Yourself

Whether for yourself or the next owner of your home, safety issues should be addressed as soon as they become apparent. These include bare electrical wires, open splices, amateur plumbing or electrical work, leaking flue pipes, carbon monoxide leaks, oil spillage, etc. We have often seen numerous small repairs done on plumbing or electrical components that were less than ideal, such as duct tape on a plumbing leak, or extension cords snaked through a wall for access in another area of the home. The buyer will often become skeptical when issues like this come to light, as he may start to think that even more problems lurk behind the walls. This discomfort with maintenance may lead to the termination of the contract. It is important to make sure that all repairs are done according to today's standards and safety recommendations in order to avoid future problems.

Part Six:

Tips and Suggestions

The Top Ten Suggestions to Ensure a Better Home Inspection

---

1. **Have your heating and cooling system serviced annually.** Most oil companies have a service contract that includes an annual maintenance checkup of your boiler or furnace. Be sure that at the time of the maintenance, the company changes any filters, cleans out the flue, supplies you with a list of parts replaced, and puts a service tag on the unit for your records. Regular maintenance is key to keeping your system in the most efficient working order.

2. **Have your septic system pumped out regularly.** People who let their septic system go for more than five years without a pump-out are asking for trouble. Ask your septic service company to send you a reminder when it is time for a scheduled pump-out. While the job is being done, ask if he will inform you of needed repairs such as broken baffles or broken covers.

3. **Don't hang around at the inspection.** More often than not, the presence of the homeowner can complicate the inspection process, causing lost time and awkward situations. If you have a licensed realtor representing you, let this professional do his or her job. Their representation is what the commission is based upon. If you feel more comfortable, leave your cell phone number so you can be contacted if any important questions come up during the inspection.

4. **Don't try to hide known defects.** While you may get away with hiding a condition from the inspector, it is unlikely. Covering over cracked tiles or rotted timbers is not usually successful, as most inspectors can see through this. The discovery of an issue that appears to have been disguised only leaves a bad taste for your buyer. The question always comes up: What else is he hiding? If you know of a defect, let your realtor know so it can be included on the list of disclosures.

5. **Have your house ready on the day of the inspection.** Put your home in its best light: Shovel walkways and the driveway of snow, clear out debris inside and outside, clean the house, and get rid of strong odors.

6. **Don't leave your animals behind at the time of the inspection.** Tying up the dog or leaving the cat behind may complicate the inspection process. Homeowners will often leave notes instructing visitors to be sure not to let the cat out. Unfortunately, the inspection means your home is being invaded by strangers, and animals can become frightened or traumatized. Either take the animals with you, or have them in a secure animal crate during the inspection so that they are safe, and as unaffected by the visitors as possible.

7. **Don't plan special events on the day of the inspection.** It is difficult to predict how much time an inspection will take, so avoid planning something that must start at a certain time, whether or not the inspection is completed. Tag sales, birthday parties, luncheons, and other social events should be rescheduled for everyone's sake.

Keep It Simple

One seller made the poor decision of holding a tag sale on the day of the scheduled inspection, which made things very difficult for all of us. In many cases, a home inspection includes the arrival of numerous parties—the real estate agents, the buyer and his or her family, the inspector, a septic company, a termite company, and possibly even a town official. This particular inspection felt like a block party, except it was tense and trying, and the buyers didn't have fun.

---

8. **Be sure that your agent has access to the home, as well as to all locked areas.** Confirm this on the morning of the inspection before you leave. Leave remote openers for the garage doors, and keys for locked closets, rooms, or outdoor buildings that will be inspected. There is nothing worse than having all the people arrive for an inspection and not being able to get into the home—yet it happens more often than you would think.

9. **Have all utilities turned on in advance.** If you are selling a seasonal property, the utilities need to be turned on for the inspection process. If it is a property that has been winterized, it is important to turn on the water a few days ahead and make sure that there are no frozen or burst pipes. Most inspectors

will not turn on main breakers or valves, as they do not want to be the one to discover major issues that need emergency attention.

10. **Don't get overanxious about the inspection.** Many people feel like they are taking a major exam when their house is scheduled for inspection. If you have taken the time to prepare your home, you can feel comfortable about the process. If you have not done anything to prepare it, no amount of worry will change what the inspector will find. In most cases, a small list of findings can be addressed through negotiations with the help of your agent. So relax on the day of the inspection, and learn from the process.

Don't Waste Everyone's Time and Your Money

Once in a while, we arrive at an inspection and no one has a key to the home. Sometimes, the inspection may have to be rescheduled (possibly at additional expense, depending on the inspection company). To avoid this frustrating experience, you should consider hiding a key and leaving a reliable contact number for your agent. In one case, our attempts to get into a home set off the alarm, which quickly brought the police to the scene. Be sure to give accurate alarm information to prevent this embarrassing situation.

Questions Frequently
Asked by
Home Buyers

———

Having completed thousands of home inspections over the past ten years, I often get the same questions from buyers over and over again. While many of the questions asked are outside of the scope of a typical home inspection, we still try to give a fair explanation so the buyer has a clear understanding of his or her concerns. Here are some of the most common questions, with our best answers.

Do you think the home is worth "X" amount of dollars? Would you buy this home?

First of all, as home inspectors, we are rarely made aware of the sales price of the home. Our job is to identify components of the home, report on areas that are problematic, and make recommendations for further evaluation where appropriate. The value of the property is the domain of the appraiser, who can give an accurate comparison assessment of the home. When buyers ask us this question, it does tell us they want to be reassured that their purchase price is fair. If you have any information, such as recent appraisals or comparative property sales, it might be helpful in reassuring your buyer about his decision to buy. Your realtor can also be of great help in this situation.

Is the home well built?

As with many questions, the answer to this is relative to the building standards at the time the home was built. An inspector will point out structural concerns and obvious defects, but "grading" the home is beyond the scope of any inspection. I will usually reassure buyers if the materials and construction techniques of the home in question are typical of the era, or surpass the standard qualities of the period. As the current owner, if you have any information pertaining to the reputation of the builder of your home, it is certainly worth passing on to your buyer, or the buyer's agent. If it is a very old or antique home, and you have some historical information, most buyers appreciate receiving that information, as well.

Is the basement wet; or, do you think it ever experienced leakage?

Most basements have experienced leaks at one time or another, and it is likely that the occupants have taken measures to correct the problem. This may include removal of damaged areas, painting over water stains, and adding drainage to divert water. The best indication of basement leakage is the word of the current owner. It is important to let your buyer know your experiences, any unusual circumstances during the time you lived in the house, and any measures you took to prevent future basement leakage. In my own home, the basement flooded once in the early eighties during an unusually bad storm. Because of this, I installed drain piping around the house, as well as downspout extensions, and the home has never had a problem in the ten years my family and I have lived there since.

Is the roof leaking? I see stains in the attic.

The older the home, the more chances are that at some time or another the roof or chimney flashing has leaked. Very often, this is the first indication to a homeowner that the roof needs to be replaced. Considering that shingles last anywhere from fifteen to twenty-five years, a seventy-five-year-old home should surely have had the roofing shingles replaced at least two times, and they may be due for replacement again. Water stains in the sheathing (the plywood that the roof shingles are nailed to) or coming down the chimney on the interior is not an automatic indication of current leakage, and as inspectors, we are trained to assess the situation at the time. If you are aware of a minor leak, it is advisable to consult with a roofing contractor to track down the source and have it repaired. It is much easier to disclose to your buyer that the chimney leaked in the past, but the flashing was replaced, thereby eliminating the leak.

Are the stains in the ceiling wet?

It is common to find minor water stains here and there on a ceiling. Very often, they are in the vicinity of a second-floor bathroom, and might have only been caused by a particularly messy kid coming out of the bath. No matter how well sealed we make the bathroom, a child playing with water can cause a leak somewhere. It may also have been caused by a short-term leak that was discovered shortly after it started, but not quite soon enough. Small stains are not usually an indication of a major problem, but when stains are large and show signs of repeated leakage, we will usually use a moisture meter to determine if the leak is active. As the homeowner, you probably know which stains in your ceiling are old and have been there for some time. You can either leave them, and try to reassure your buyer that they are from a past leakage, or seal them with a stain killer and repaint the ceiling. Your decision will be based upon the extent of staining and the concern it might cause.

Can I take out that wall or post?
Can we add a second story?

As home inspectors, we are not in the business of giving advice on practical engineering issues. These kinds of inquiries require further evaluation from a structural engineer, and the relatively short amount of time that we spend in a home is not adequate to determine load capacities, bearing walls, etc. If you have retained the services of an engineer at one time to explore the possibility of additions, either out or up, you may want to share this with your buyer.

Is there mold present?

As we pointed out earlier, mold testing can give different results at different times, as it is affected by so many factors, including humidity, temperature, or air conditioning. There are home inspectors who may test for mold, and there are companies that specialize in air and surface testing. The best advice here is to try to reduce the potential for mold to grow. Try to improve areas where dampness is a problem, especially bathrooms, by installing fans for venting, moisture barriers on dirt floors, repairing leakage of roofs and windows, and increasing ventilation in attics.

Do you smell that damp smell or animal odor?

Smells can be a big turnoff to a buyer. Having inspected homes laced with cat urine so strong it would burn your eyes, and bad food odors that would turn your stomach, I cannot blame a buyer for turning and walking away. If your home has had pets, it may be worthwhile to have the carpets and floors cleaned by a professional company. Be sure to change the cat litter prior to home showings, and vacuum the floors as well. Be aware that smells you have become immune to are very apparent to someone walking into your house for the first time. Don't keep piles of dirty clothes around, and clean the refrigerator regularly while your home is on the market. Be sure to do all of this before you try to cover odors with air freshener sprays and plug-ins. Sometimes the combination of bad odors masked by a sweet aroma only makes the situation worse!

How old do you think the furnace,
air conditioner, roof, or addition are?

When available, we note the age of an appliance, mechanical item, or structure if it is noted through the serial numbers or stamped date on the unit. Many appliances may not have this information readily available, so the best an inspector can do is to estimate the age based on several factors. It is quite helpful when a seller has documentation to show the age of the item or structure, or offers firsthand knowledge.

What does the water treatment system do?

Many private wells have some sort of water treatment system installed, and it is beyond the scope of a home inspection to determine the adequacy, reliability, or operation of such a system. Be sure to have ready any information regarding your system so you can pass it on to the buyer. Let them know if it is a rental unit, if it was installed by you and you maintain it, or if a company services it on a regular maintenance schedule. Have records of service, as well as the name of the company and contact information, ready to give to your buyer.

Is there asbestos or lead in the house?

Asbestos and lead content are environmental concerns and beyond the scope of a standard home inspection, though some state regulations may differ on this. Be sure to check with your local regulations about environmental testing. While further testing is required for a definitive answer in most cases, there are situations when the presence of asbestos or lead is clearly known. In these cases, an inspector will flag it and recommend abatement by a professional company. If it is a case of a possibility or probability of the presence of a hazardous material, an inspector will recommend further evaluation. Either way, it may delay the finalization of your sales contract, and it may be to your advantage to address environmental concerns prior to listing your home.

Are there termites?

Some people have wisely had their homes inspected by an exterminating company prior to listing their home. Sellers are often surprised when evidence of active termites is found in their home, having felt confident that they would have noticed it. While some evidence of termites is obvious, it often takes an experienced person to find the less obvious signs. Very often this is worse, as the termites have gone unnoticed for far too long. Usually for a cost of less than a hundred dollars, it is far less stressful on the seller and the buyer to have a termite inspection done shortly before listing your home. If you have had regular preventive treatments, be sure to have your documentation on hand, as it may save you the cost of treatment if old damage is identified at the inspection.

Is there hardwood flooring under the wall-to-wall carpeting?

It is not always possible for an inspector to determine what type of floor is beneath a carpet. In fact, it is rarely possible, unless a corner of carpet is loose or missing. If you know what is underneath the carpet, let the buyer know, especially if it is hardwood flooring. Hardwood floors will add value to your home, particularly if they are in fairly good condition.

The water pressure seems low; do you think there is a problem?

Low water pressure can be caused by several things, making it difficult for an inspector to determine the problem during a one-time visit. One of the first things you can do is remove aerators and screens from faucet heads and clean away any sediment. These devices are usually threaded on the end of the faucet, where the water flows out. You may need a pair of pliers to do this if the aerator has not been removed in some time. It is hard to believe, but a little sand in an aerator can slow water down to a mere trickle. When doing a water test, the aerator is removed to draw the sample, and I have surprised many a seller by the increase in pressure after replacing the clean aerator. Low water pressure can also be the result of a tired pump or a problem with an expansion tank. At any rate, if the pressure in your home is notoriously low, you might want to consult with a plumber to see if you can do anything to improve it. Buyers become anxious when the flow is reduced, and may fear that it is due to a lack of adequate water in the well.

Are those serious cracks in the sheetrock wall or ceiling?

Cracks concern almost all buyers, and serious ones concern inspectors. Many cracks may have been caused by a lack of drywall fasteners, causing uneven drying, wood shrinkage, or poor tape joints. Repairing even minor cracks may make for a smoother inspection process. If you see cracks that are larger than ¼ inch, further exploration by a building contractor may be needed.

Are those cracks in the foundation serious?

Any large crack indicating movement is an obvious red flag that should be addressed by a structural engineer. Small shrinkage cracks can be sealed by the homeowner, or there are companies that specialize in sealing concrete.

Are the cracks in the floor slab serious?

The floor slab is not usually a structural component, so minor cracks are not considered serious. With that said, a crack that is near a structural column may be considered a problem by virtue of its locale. This would require the advice of a professional engineer or qualified builder. Once again, sealing these cracks will give a better presentation.

Where do you think the property lines are?

Most inspectors are not surveyors, and will not be able to give any information on this. If you have a survey map of the property, leave it out for display and show your realtor. Better yet, walk your agent around the property when you initially list your property. Many town halls are working hard to compile accurate databases on property information, so if a survey has been done on the property, the information may have been filed at your local town hall. Today, with the accessibility of the Internet, some information is even available online through the use of Geographic Information Systems (GIS). Check with your municipality for information.

How long do you think that roof / dishwasher / septic system will last?

An inspector does not have a crystal ball that tells him the future, and most people know that if something is ready to break down, it will do so at the most inconvenient time! Some items have generally accepted life spans, and an inspector might point out that a specific appliance has outlived its life expectancy. This is a good indication that the buyer needs to budget for replacement soon. If you have several items in your home that have gone beyond the typical life span, it might be prudent to replace the neediest ones before the sale. Consult with your realtor on the advisability of this in relation to your sale price.

What about the alarm system?

Most inspections will not evaluate an alarm, as it is generally a low-voltage system. If your alarm system is active, it is suggested that you take the time to familiarize your buyer with the operation of the unit and any service contracts.

What kind of bug is that?

As inspectors, we see many types of insects. However, we are mostly concerned with wood-boring insects, which include termites, powder post beetles, carpenter ants, and carpenter bees. We have discussed these insects in more detail in the chapter on basements. It is advisable to have an exterminator come to your home if you have a chronic problem with any type of insect. Inspecting a home with live evidence of cockroaches, rodents, wasps, bees, or fleas is not a pleasant experience for the inspector or for the buyer. Some buyers become very disturbed at the sight of such bugs, so getting rid of them is important.

Carpenter bees can cause serious damage to a home.
If you see them around yours, you may want to call an
exterminator before the inspection.

Are those animal droppings?

Mice can make it through incredibly small openings, so it is not surprising to find evidence of these critters in most homes. Their droppings are tiny and often go unnoticed by the homeowner. Larger droppings are always a concern because it is not always clear what kind of animal is sharing your home. It is, of course, important to get rid of unwanted animals prior to listing your home, but it is just as important to get rid of the evidence left behind.

Can you believe people live like this?

While it is common sense to have a clean house for the inspection, we have seen some nasty, messy situations in our inspection process. Even though some homes in this condition still sell, you are limiting yourself to fewer buyers who are willing to overlook these conditions. In addition, a poor presentation can negatively affect the price you get for your home. A clean, well-organized home is much easier to present and sell.

Do you know where the well is located, and how deep it is?

Please refer to the chapter on plumbing for more detailed information about wells. While the question is sometimes easy to answer, it is often the realtor and seller that will provide this information. Some wells are hidden in overgrowth or even under the ground surface. If you have information about the location and depth of the well, be sure to provide it to your buyer.

Does the pool or hot tub work properly?

Many inspectors do not inspect these items as part of a general inspection, so if you have any service records, winterization information, or warranty paperwork, pass it on to the buyer.

Is there damage behind the loose tiles in the tub or shower?

When loose or cracked tiles are discovered in a bathroom or shower, I always caution a prospective buyer of the possibility of hidden damage. The inspection process is limited to a visual inspection, not allowing us to dismantle anything, so the possibility of hidden damage will often scare a buyer away. It is easier to repair these items prior to a sale rather than take a chance on losing a sale due to an unknown factor.

How much will it cost to repair or replace the roof / furnace / electrical service / termite damage, etc.?

In most cases, it is impossible to answer this question without further information. It is best to consult with a qualified contractor and get a professional estimate (or several bids) on work to be performed. If an issue is being negotiated between you and the buyer, each of you may want to get your own independent estimate for the fairest approach to the problem. To get an idea of approximate repair/improvement costs, see the last chapter.

Do you know a good builder, or do you have a list of dependable contractors?

Most professional inspectors will not recommend contractors, so as to avoid conflict-of-interest issues. However, if you have a contractor or plumber that has been dependable, you, as the seller, may want to share the information with your buyer.

Does the property flood?

As inspectors, we try to assess the adequacy of the grade to determine the probability of water concerns, but we are not expected to be aware of flood zones. As the seller, you should disclose any known information regarding flooding, and the town should have maps that indicate the flood zones. Very often, a mortgage company will require flood insurance if a property lies within a flood zone.

What kind of wood or material is that?

Some buyers are very interested in special woods or materials in your home, so if you know the floors are cherry, the cabinets are walnut, or the trim is oak, share this information with your buyer.

Does the inspection serve as a guarantee or warranty on the home, or any of the components (such as the boiler or the appliances)?

Inspection reports are not a guarantee or warranty of any kind; rather, the report is just an inspector's opinion on the condition of the home on the day of the inspection. This is an important point for you, the seller, to understand, as it impacts your sale (or your monetary compensation). It is to your benefit to clearly understand all the duties of those involved in the sale of your home, including the realtor, the inspector, the lawyer, and the appraiser.

Tips on Basic Maintenance and Preparation

Now that you have given your home a thorough inspection, you probably have a substantial to-do list. Of course, you can always hire someone to do the work for you, but you may spend just as much time searching for the right person—or more likely, people—to complete the work as it would take to tackle much of it yourself. There are many how-to books available online or in home centers, but we want to summarize a general maintenance list, along with tips on completing some of the basic tasks without using specialized, expensive tools. If you're operating on a limited budget, these tips should go a long way toward increasing your profits, while reducing inspection issues. As an experienced builder/remodeler and the past owner of numerous investment properties, I have used these techniques when preparing a property for presentation.

Exterior Maintenance— The First Impression

Painting

As mentioned before, the condition of the exterior often makes the first impression on anyone arriving at your home for a showing. It is important to enhance the "curb appeal" of the house. There are a few new cable TV programs devoted to improving the appeal of your home, such as *Curb Appeal* and *Designed to Sell*. Check your local listings for times. A fresh coat of paint goes a long way in accomplishing this. If you have a two-story home, or higher, it may be worthwhile to have a professional painter complete the project, as ladders or staging may be needed and injury could result if you are not adept with heights. Be aware that homes built prior to 1978 could contain lead paint, which is considered a hazardous material. There are specific guidelines in dealing with lead paint, so be sure to consult with a professional before disturbing the surface. This could also be a health hazard to you and your loved ones, so don't take any chances. If you are sure that the paint is not lead-based, it is important to make sure loose and peeling paint is scraped, and that the surface is clean and dry prior to recoating.

Power washing can be helpful in preparing the surface. If you don't own a power washer, you can usually rent one at your local hardware store or rental center. It is advantageous to paint with the same color that is already on the house, as fewer coats should be needed. If the preexisting color is unusual or uncommon, it may be worthwhile to consider a neutral color, as it would appeal to a larger audience.

There are two main types of exterior paints: latex-based, which can be cleaned up with water, and oil-based, which requires mineral spirits for cleanup. There are also stains that come in many colors and finishes, which can be applied to exterior wood siding if it has not been painted. Stains are oil-based and can be translucent (where the grain shows through the stain somewhat) or opaque (solid-color stain). Your local paint dealer can better assist you in making the proper choice.

After scraping, you may have some bare spots that require spot painting with a primer, or undercoat paint, to seal them. As with any project, there are several ways the paint can be applied: by brush, pad, sprayer, or roller. Each method has its advantages and disadvantages. It is best to paint in low humidity with the temperature above sixty degrees, and the surface you are painting should also be above sixty degrees. If you are using a spray painter, never spray on very windy days.

Cleaning and sealing decks

Decks are usually constructed of moisture-resistant wood or manufactured composite material. The most common woods utilized may include pressure-treated pine, cedar, mahogany, redwood, and some species of fir. If your deck is painted and the paint is peeling or in poor condition, it may be time to clean and repaint it. There are special deck paints available at paint stores or home centers. Just ask the specialist in the paint section for assistance.

It is important to make sure that the surface is free of peeling paint (it must be scraped if needed), clean, and dry prior to recoating. There are cleaning solutions available that have been specially formulated to clean and kill any organic growth on the deck surface. Be sure to follow the directions on the container for the best results. A power washer can sometimes be utilized, but be careful not to damage the wood, as the water stream can be powerful enough to dig out chunks of wood. The same process holds true for a natural wood surface; you should clean the surface and coat with your choice of a clear preservative or transparent or opaque stain. Many buyers prefer a natural surface, so it may be wise to stick with the natural, as it can always be stained by the new buyer if desired. Be sure to replace any rotted or damaged boards that you note after the deck has been cleaned. If you are unsure of what type of paint or stain to use on the surface (or what type of cleaner), it may be worthwhile to take a picture of your deck and consult with your local paint store specialist for recommendations on products, procedures, and materials to use.

Sealing cracks and top-coating the driveway

Do-it-yourself driveway repairs and coating can usually be accomplished without costly tools or technical experience. There are numerous crack-filling compounds for various crack widths, along with cold-patch asphalt for larger holes. The top coat is usually applied with a large squeegee, a tool with a flat rubber edge designed to evenly spread a liquid, covering the entire surface. Tools required usually include a broom, a squeegee, a trowel, and possibly a caulking gun for some products. There are different grades of top-coating materials available, so it would be best if you consulted with your home center expert for advice on application and proper coating for your situation. If your driveway is beyond repair with the use of these common coatings, an asphalt contractor should be consulted. The high cost of repaving your driveway may not be recoverable in your sales price, so discuss any large investment such as this with your agent prior to committing to the job.

Sealing cracks and top-coating concrete surfaces

Most home centers now have a whole section dedicated to crack and concrete surface repairs. Smaller cracks can be filled with an appropriate mortar filler or patching compound. Skimming a patching compound with a trowel can level larger raised portions. There are now some top-coat masonry products that can be applied once the cracks, voids, and deteriorated spots have been patched. With any of these products, always read the specific directions on the label, as there are several products available today, each of which may have a specific use. If your walkway is in very poor condition, hiring a mason contractor may be necessary.

Repairing and replacing storm windows

Most storm windows today are made out of aluminum frames, though some very old homes still have the wooden storm windows. Most inspectors will note if there are any missing screens or glass inserts, so you may want to go around and make a list of missing units. Then look in your basement, attic, garage, or shed to see if the old inserts or frames are in storage. Most glass companies will replace the glass in the frame if you drop it off at their place of business, and they will often be able to replace the screening where needed. If you are patient and have confidence in yourself, screens can usually be repaired by removing the plastic spline (a long, thin piece of rubber), cutting new screening to size, and then holding the screen taut prior to reinstalling the spline with a special screen tool that looks like a pizza cutter.

The tracks of the aluminum storms and screens can often become pitted, so applying a lubricant may help their operation. Over the years, the inserts may become jammed into the tracks, testing the extent of your patience at removal and reinstallation. After completing these repairs, clean the windows for an impressive presentation.

Replacing glass and glazing single-pane, wood sash windows

Single-pane windows are held in place on older sashes with the use of "points" and putty, or "glazing." In time, the glazing will dry out and become loose, brittle, and cracked. Repairing this is quite simple, though tedious. The tools you will need include a putty knife, glazing compound, glazer's points (sharp pieces of metal which help hold the glass in), and linseed oil. You want to scrape away all loose putty, removing any broken glass (be sure to wear gloves to prevent serious cuts or injury), and apply some linseed oil to the dry wood (this helps the putty stick). Smooth a thin layer of glazing compound over the linseed oil. Next, insert the new glass (usually cut ⅛ inch smaller on each side), gently pressing it into the glazing compound and apply the glazing points with a screwdriver (see picture). You are now ready to angle the putty knife and smooth

The first step in glazing windows is to assemble your materials.
Here is a putty knife and glazing compound.

Make sure to remove all loose and cracked
putty before applying the new glazing.

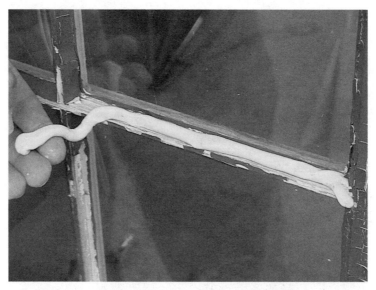

Apply the glazing compound in thin strips.

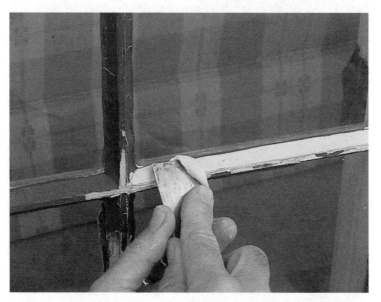

Using a putty knife, press the glazing compound into the window
seam until it is smooth and the glass is securely in place.

an evenly beveled bead around the square or rectangle. The compound can be painted
once it is sufficiently dried, usually after a twenty-four-hour period. Be sure to wash
your hands thoroughly afterwards, as you don't want any lead dust to be ingested from
old window surfaces.

Repairing Thermopane windows

Unfortunately for your pocketbook, double-pane windows need to be repaired by a qualified glass company, as the windows need to be properly sealed to prevent fogging, which is caused by the presence of moisture in the space between the panes. You may be able to keep the cost down by removing the sash and bringing it to the glass company for repair at their factory. If windows have fogged, be sure to check if there is a guarantee that could be utilized to minimize or totally cover the cost of the repair.

Repairing exterior doors

Wood doors should have a good coat of paint, stain, or clear polyurethane to keep them from getting weather damaged. If the door has cracking in its panels, is warped, or has extensive rot, it probably needs to be replaced. If the lockset does not function properly, or is worn or broken, a replacement set can be purchased and installed. You will find that there are a number of different types, qualities, and brands. Each individual lock company has directions enclosed to make the job fairly straightforward. Many exterior doors have an adjustable sill to improve the weather resistant quality. You will notice three or four brass screws at the base that can be adjusted to raise or lower this sill. Adjust until the door closes easily, yet does not allow a draft (or light) at the base. While you have the screwdriver in hand, you can check the hinges to make sure they are all tight. If the casings or jambs are rotted, they should be replaced, though this may be a job for a carpenter, depending on your experience. If any glass inserts are broken, they should be replaced now. Depending on the style of door, you may be able to do it yourself, or you may need a glass company to install new glass.

Maintaining metal doors

Metal doors often rust with age and exposure to excessive moisture. If the surface is not too badly rusted, a light sanding and application of a rust-inhibiting paint may do the trick. Examine the doorjambs and casings for wood rot and replace as necessary.

Sliding doors

Sliding doors can sometimes roll with great difficulty. The first step is to clean the tracks, lubricate them, and attempt to adjust the rollers. Usually, there is a small hole at the bottom of the door unit that either a Phillips-head or slotted screwdriver will fit into. It will probably require a fairly small screwdriver, and be prepared—visibility is limited! By turning the screwdriver one way or the other, it will make the door go up or down. After a small adjustment, test the door by sliding it back and forth to see if it has improved. If not, give it a little more adjustment until you get it to where it works easily. Hopefully, this will improve the ease with which the doors slide, but if not, replacing the rollers may be the only alternative. If you decide to replace the rollers, two people need to lift the door up into the upper track, while sliding the bottom of the door straight out away from the jamb, and then lowering the upper end. The roller assembly can then be removed with a screwdriver. Take this to your local hardware store to match up the correct replacement roller. There are many different types of rollers and doors, so you want to be sure you have the correct one to avoid a frustrating day! Reassembly should be fairly straightforward, and you will be pleased with the results.

Cleaning gutters and installing extension drains

Gutters are installed on many homes, except in extreme northern areas where snow and ice reduce their benefits. Cleaning gutters is one of the most important tasks to keep up with, as this will keep large amounts of water away from your home, keeping basement leakage and rot at a minimum. This can, however, be a dangerous task if not done with caution. When using ladders, be mindful of the location of electrical wires to avoid electrocution. If your home has very high gutters, or a very steep roof, it may be best to hire this job out. If you are able to safely access the gutters, a hose with a spray jet can be helpful in forcing debris and packed leaves out of the elbows of downspouts. Other helpful items include gloves, a pail, and a sturdy ladder. Make sure the ladder is secure at the base and on a level surface prior to going up the rungs.

In many cases, it is a good idea to add extension drains to the ends of the downspouts in order to keep water away from the foundation of the home. Many home centers now have extensions that easily fit over the opening of most downspouts, and are made of flexible accordion plastic that can be stretched out and bent to guide the water to a specific location. Some people will just add the extensions and let them sit on top of the ground, while others prefer to dig a shallow trench, lay the extensions in the trench, and then cover them, so that they are not visible.

Maintaining manual garage doors

We recommend that if an adjustment or replacement of garage-door hardware is needed, a garage-door specialist do this, as the springs or cables can be dangerous. Lubricating the tracks with grease, such as white lithium grease, is advised if the operation is stiff or difficult. The lower seal and the seals at the sides should be tight and in good condition. Replacing the weather stripping can usually be done without too much difficulty. If the weather stripping is attached to a wood strip, home stores usually carry replacement strips, as well as standard rubber gasket stock. If paint is peeling on wood panels, they may need to be scraped and repainted.

Fixing loose insulation

Fallen or loose fiberglass insulation, whether in crawl spaces, basements, or attics, is a common defect noted in inspection reports. An important safety consideration when working with fiberglass is to be sure to wear protective clothing, including gloves, safety goggles, and a respirator or mask over your nose and mouth. Most

Make sure to install batt insulation with the paper facing toward
the living space, and the insulation facing you.

home centers sell lightweight, one-piece disposable suits that can be thrown away when done. These work very well in less than ideal areas such as crawl spaces. Generally, the tools you will need include a utility knife, a square staple gun, and staples.

Insulation usually comes faced or unfaced, which is when the paper is attached to one side. The widths available are either 15-inch or 23-inch, and you buy the width that best fits your floor-joist spacing. The material is usually bought in an 8-foot length or roll, in "batt" form (where the insulation is adhered on one side to a paper or foil for installation purposes). One of the most common errors made by homeowners is to put insulation in backwards. The facing, or paper, should be placed *toward* the living space, so when you are doing a crawl space, you will not see any paper when you are finished, as it is placed against the floor. Securing the insulation in overhead locations (such as crawl spaces) can be accomplished by the use of metal rods (lightning rods) that are measured and precut for typical floor-joist spacing. Some people will make use of chicken wire, as this also allows the insulation to breathe. Basically, measure the length and width of open spaces to determine the size of insulation to be cut using your utility knife. Be mindful of any holes or stains in the old insulation, as this can be an indication of rats or mice. If that is the case, an exterminator should be consulted to take care of that issue.

Interior Maintenance

Windows

Replacing rope balances Many older homes were built with the old-style windows that utilized ropes and balances to keep the sash from slamming down. The ropes often deteriorate with age, or simply break, making the windows difficult to operate, or dangerous when there is nothing to hold them up. It is possible to replace these ropes, usually by removing one side of the window stop (this is the thin vertical length of wood that holds the window sash in place and acts like a guide for the window to move up and down) that may be screwed or nailed in place. Gently remove the sash (the framework that holds the panes of glass) by pulling out the side that had the stop removed. The ropes are knotted in each sash and can be removed at this time. The window weights, usually made of heavy metal, are located within the jamb on each side of the window. Look carefully for what appears to be a wood patch in the jamb, and carefully remove it, trying not to damage the wood. Now you can measure the length of the sash rope, cut new ones, and install them by threading the new rope through the top pulley, pulling it down and then securing the new rope to the weight. Your local hardware store should be able to direct you to the correct rope for this purpose. Once the weight is tied on, reinstall all the pieces and check the window for smooth operation. If necessary, adjust the knots accordingly. If all the windows are the same size in your home, the same rope measurement can be used for other broken sashes.

Fixing vinyl sashes Vinyl windows have become very popular in the last thirty years or so, and they also may need some localized repairs. Common defects may include fogged glass, cracked glass, broken balances, or broken locks. The sashes can usually be removed and taken to a window-repair shop for glass repairs. Hardware repairs can be more of a challenge, as you may have to examine the complete window carefully, looking for the name of the manufacturer. Unfortunately, there have been many vinyl window manufacturers that have gone out of business, and many windows have no identifying labels. If you do find a name, you may be able to go on the Internet and track down replacement parts. If the unit is in need of multiple repairs, it may be best to replace the whole unit.

Maintaining aluminum windows One of the common failures of aluminum windows is fogging of the glass, which is again a job for a glass-repair company. On sliding windows, the sash can usually be removed by gently lifting up the sash and pulling the lower half out. The rollers may become difficult to operate, so first try to clean out the track with a vacuum and cloth or brush, and then apply a lubricant to the rollers. The metal can usually be spray-painted if the glass portion is taped and covered, to help keep the overspray off the glass.

Doors
Fixing hollow-core doors The most common defects found on hollow-core doors are the de-lamination of the door surface, and holes in the door. Unfortunately, when these doors are treated without care, such as someone kicking against a door, the thin laminated surface gives way and collapses in. In addition, when these

doors are in a very humid environment, such as a wet basement or poorly ventilated bathroom, the door warps easily, causing the layers to start separating. If either of these conditions are attended to early, you may be able to patch with a wood patch, and restain or repaint the doors. Large holes or big pieces peeling off usually warrant replacing the door.

Fixing bifold doors It seems that a large number of bifold doors work poorly or are completely off the track at the top of the jamb. This is probably because many people don't know that there is hardware that can be adjusted, nor do they know where to make the adjustment. On most bifold doors, the adjustment hardware is located at the stationary part of the door. At the top and bottom of the door, closest to the side or doorjamb, are screws that can be tightened or loosened. By positioning the door close to the jamb, at both the top and bottom (make sure the distances are equal, and the pin at center top of door is in track before tightening the screw), and then tightening down on the screws, your door should open and close freely and stay in the track.

Patching drywall

Small holes and indentations Small holes can usually be spackled with the use of a putty or taping knife. If the surface is raised, a light tap with a hammer should indent the area prior to coating it. Spackling compound can be purchased at most home centers, hardware, and paint stores, in a variety of sizes. In some cases, two coats may be required, as the material shrinks as it dries. Once the compound is fully dry, a light sanding with 150-grit sandpaper will provide a clean, smooth area, ready for finishing with paint or wallpaper.

Larger holes Large holes are a little more difficult to patch, as the compound needs something to cling to as it dries, and it is not strong material. You should cut a piece of wood large enough to fit behind the hole, but small enough to slide into the hole at an angle. Using a long screw in the center of the wood to hold it into place, install screws through the sheetrock and into the wood backing. The wood backing should now be securely held in place, and the area can be filled with a small piece of drywall, cut to size. Use tape and two or three layers of compound to fill the seam areas and screw holes, and smooth as necessary. Another method commonly used is to crumple some newspaper, jam it in the wall to fill the cavity, and coat the area with a plaster patch compound that dries quickly. The area can now be lightly sanded and coated with a spackle compound to obtain a smooth surface. For very large areas, it might be more reasonable to cut the drywall from stud to stud and screw in another drywall piece (to size), finishing with compound and light sanding as described above. Visit http://www.repair-home.com/how_to/repair_holes_in_drywall.htm for more instructions on fixing large holes in sheetrock.

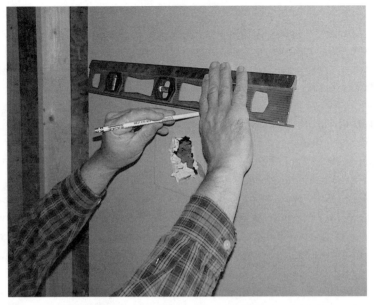

Measure a rectangle slightly bigger than the hole you wish to patch.

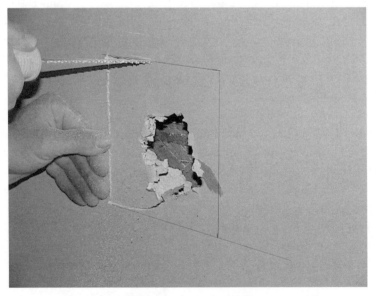

Carefully cut away the sheetrock along the measured lines.

Using this hole as your guide, cut a piece of wood that is
large enough to fit behind the hole.

Slide the wood backing into the hole and
use a long screw in the center of the wood to hold it into place.

Install screws on either side of the hole through the sheetrock,
into the wood backing.

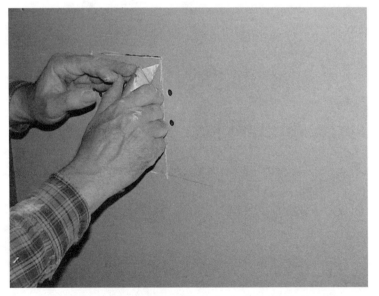

Now you are ready to fill the hole with drywall.

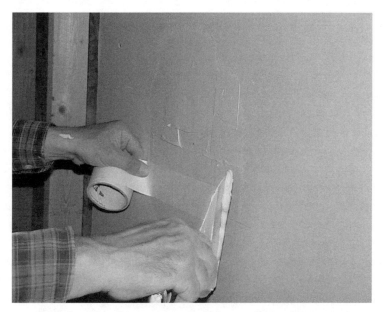

Once the drywall is in place, the hole may be taped over and
smoothed with wall compound. If you do this right,
you won't even know there was a hole there.

Sealing drywall stains Prior water stains can be a real eyesore, and an unnecessary concern for both buyers and inspectors if the leak source has been corrected. As long as the cause (such as an old plumbing or roof leak) is no longer an issue, the stain should be sealed with a paint sealer, which can be found at most paint stores. This sealer is designed to be applied to the stain and helps reduce the chance of the stain bleeding through. Unfortunately, once applied, the entire ceiling or wall will probably need painting. Consult with your paint/hardware specialist for sealant recommendations.

Repairing minor drywall cracks Quite often over the years, minor hairline cracks can develop in ceilings and walls (often above doorways), usually resulting from wood shrinkage, earth movement below the home, vehicle traffic if you are close to a busy road, and home settling. If any of the cracks are deep and wide, ⅛ of an inch or greater, and you are experiencing doors sticking or floor movement, you should contact a professional contractor or engineer for advice. Smaller cracks are common in most homes and can be filled with a taping compound or spackling compound obtained at a home center. It may take a few coats to take care of these cracks, as the material shrinks when it dries. The process is very similar to the process as outlined above, though in some cases, it might be necessary to V-groove the crack. You can accomplish this through the use of a standard, pointed can opener, the kind used to open juice cans. Run the pointed edge along the crack, which will give you a tapered groove that allows the compound to stick. In some cases it may also be necessary to use tape to blend the areas. Once dry, apply additional coats of compound as needed prior to sanding. A light sanding between coats will give a smooth finished product, but remember to wear a nose-and-mouth mask when sanding for your health and safety.

Repairing seams Seams can often be identified by the very straight line, and slightly lifted surface, that makes a wall look like it has a hole in it. This is the paper tape that has lifted and pulled away from the wall. If you have areas like this, it will be necessary to peel away any loose tape, clean the finish below, smooth a thin layer of compound on the wall in this area, and apply a new length of fresh tape onto the wet compound. Be sure that there are no air bubbles behind this tape, as that is what usually causes the tape to pull away in the first place. Once securely in place and dried, apply one or two more coats and sand the area to smooth it prior to finishing with paint.

Repairing minor cracks or holes in plaster Much of the same information pertaining to filling drywall cracks and holes applies to plaster walls, with a few changes. In older homes, plaster walls were created by applying the wet plaster to thin strips of wood call lathing strips (many small horizontal strips of wood with narrow spaces between). It is not uncommon to find these walls cracked with large chunks missing. It is almost always necessary to V-groove the cracks, and in some cases, the loose adjacent pieces of plaster may need to be removed. There are special plaster patching compounds available at paint stores, hardware stores, and most home centers that work better than drywall compound. They are formulated to set quickly and can fill larger gaps with fewer coats between sanding. A mesh tape is also available that helps hold the plaster patch in the gap. Check with your paint specialist at your hardware store for products and tools available for repairs to plaster.

Repairing textured surfaces Many ceilings have some sort of a texture finish, and when damaged, it can be difficult to blend the new finish with the old. Some stores now stock various spray-on textures that can be helpful when used according to the directions. You can also purchase a sand paint, which may be useful in matching some textures. Swirl finishes can be very difficult to duplicate as you may need some artful dexterity. If you are not having much luck, you can consider retexturing the whole ceiling, or hiring a professional drywall contractor who is familiar with texture coatings or finishes.

Painting the interior Interior paint can be applied by brush, roller, pad, or sprayer. The most common type of interior paint used is latex, which is a water-based paint that can be cleaned up with water. Latex paints can be purchased in several finishes from glossy to flat, depending on the desired effect. High-gloss paints will show wall imperfections more than a flat paint, so this is a consideration when deciding what finish to use. The most important factor in painting is the preparation of the surface, as described above, and cleaning the surface prior to applying paint. If your home was built before 1978, it may contain lead paint, so be sure to refer to the environmental hazards section for safety precautions.

Some tools that will be helpful include a sturdy stepladder, drop cloths, painters' tape, and good brushes and rollers. Be sure to have the paint store mix the paint thoroughly with an electric shaker, and if it has been some time since this has been done, bring it back to the place of purchase for a quick reshake. Most stores will gladly provide this service for you, and it surely beats a lengthy stir. It is usually advised to start with the ceiling and then work your way to the walls. Applying painters' tape to the trim can be helpful if your hand is not too steady for cutting in trim or around windows. Be sure to get a trim tape that is appropriate for the area you are taping, so as not to pull away part of the wall with tape not designed for walls. Your paint store can help you choose the proper tape and brushes for the task.

Floors

Maintaining wood floors Many home buyers feel that wood floors are definitely a positive aspect of a home, and nicely finished floors always impress a potential buyer. If the clear-coat finish is slightly scratched or dull, a good cleaning with an appropriate wood product, such as Murphy Oil Soap Wood Cleaner or Butler Wood Floor Cleaner, and a single application of polyurethane will usually be sufficient to give a nice finish and bring out the beauty of the grain. If the floors are badly scratched, they may need sanding. Machines can be rented to sand floors yourself, but they can be difficult to use as they are heavy and can cause damage to a floor if you are not skilled. If you haven't used a floor drum sander before, it may be better to hire a floor sanding company, as the gouges the sander could create may be worse than the stains or scratches that you are trying to remove. I have recently seen some smaller machines that oscillate (the head spins around), and these appear to be more forgiving of a slip of the hand when sanding. For an amateur operator, we recommend you consult with the rental center when deciding which machine to use. It is also important when using a floor sander to start with a coarse grit and work your way down to a fine grit. Typically, you would start sanding in a back-and-forth motion, in the general direction of the grain of the wood. Once the floor has been sanded and well cleaned of all dust, several coats of clear polyurethane finish can be applied. A light hand sanding and dust cleanup prior to the final coat will give a nice smooth finish. Remember, high-gloss finishes will reveal more imperfections of the wood as well as the quality of the sanding job.

Fixing ceramic tile Ceramic tile defects include cracks, loose or missing grout, loose tiles, or soft areas in the floor. The latter is a more significant problem, as loose tiles need to be removed and, ideally, the soft material below replaced prior to reinstalling the tile. This may include patching the subflooring so that the area is firm and level to the bottom plane of the adjacent tiles. You may have to pull up several extra tiles around the area to be able to provide an even surface. The other problem with this kind of patch is having enough replacement tiles. Hopefully you have extra tiles from the original installation so that the match is exact. It is quite difficult to match older tiles, not only for color, but also for texture.

Other tile problems include loose grout, which can be scraped clean and re-grouted. It is likely that the newly applied grout will be a slightly different color due to the aging and fading of the old grout. In this case, thoroughly clean the entire floor and spread the grout over all the tiles, hopefully ending up with a thin layer on top of the old grout. This should give you a fresh coat of clean grout lines. There are grouting tools to apply the grout, as well as special sponges used to wipe away the haze when cleaning up after the job. Cracked tiles can sometimes be chipped out and replaced, but again, be sure you have a close tile match. Sometimes, the tub surround may only need the grout cleaned. There are several commercial products available for this task. If you discover some soft areas, it is important to address this with repair and replacement as described above.

Repairing vinyl flooring Sheet vinyl flooring often peels up at the seams and edges with age and use. If this has occurred, clean or vacuum the space below the lifted areas and apply a vinyl floor adhesive. Follow directions on waiting time, but when appropriate, smooth the area flat with the use of a rolling pin. You can also put some weights, such as bricks, on the surface to hold it down. If the surface is faded, stripping and waxing may improve the look. Cigarette burn holes can sometimes be repaired if you have a small remnant from the original installation. By overlaying a piece and meticulously matching the pattern, you can cut out a piece with a sharp knife, cutting through both the new layer and the layer beneath. This will give you edges that will match perfectly once the burned piece below is removed. Apply glue and add a weight to hold the new piece in place. If you are very careful, you should be able to cut along a line in the design of the vinyl, so as to camouflage the line of the cut.

Cleaning the carpet The least expensive method of cleaning a carpet may be to rent a carpet cleaner. Stains can usually be removed with powerful stain removers, and pet odors can often be neutralized with specially formulated solutions. These will probably be on display at the store where you rent the carpet machine. If not, look in your hardware store or home center.

General cleaning tips

Windows As we have mentioned before, cleaning windows will give a much nicer presentation and is a relatively inexpensive task. Depending on the number, size, and height of the windows, you may want to use a squeegee. Some people swear by the use of crumpled newspaper (no streaks) for cleaning windows, along with a glass cleaner, while others will use paper towels. Mixing a solution of ammonia and water is less expensive than a prepared glass cleaner, but can bother some people when used inside. Whatever you use, be sure the area is well ventilated as you work.

Siding Exterior siding can be cleaned with a power washer or with a special brush that can be installed on your household hose that may work adequately. If the siding is badly stained, there are a number of specially formulated cleaning solutions that can be applied to help lift off the dirt and stains. Be sure to read the directions before applying and note whether the cleaning solution is for vinyl, aluminum, or wood siding.

Caulking tubs, floors, windows, and doors Keeping water out of cracks and crevices is important, as this prevents wood rot or deterioration to framing, insulation, and finished surfaces. Areas that require caulking include the edges around windows and doors, and around any protrusions in the exterior walls or roof surfaces, bathroom areas, and counter and sink areas. Basically, any area where water is utilized, you should look closely for voids and caulk as necessary. When purchasing caulk, you will find that there are many choices from silicone caulk to acrylic, each with specific uses and advantages. You can find out more information on caulk properties and uses at the Web site: http://www.factsfacts.com/MyHomeRepair/caulk.htm.

Some caulking tubes are designed to fit into a caulking gun, while some tubes can be applied by squeezing with your hand or fingers. Prior to caulking any area, it is important to remove any loose or damaged caulk. Then, take a sharp knife and cut a small angled piece off at the tip of the caulking tube. Remember, you can always cut off more, but if the opening is too big, you cannot reduce that size, so start small and work your way up. With gradual pressure, push or drag the tube across the void to be filled. If needed, you can wet your finger and lightly drag it over the area to smooth the finish. If you are not sure about the type of caulk to use, consult with your local paint store or home center.

Part Seven:

The Next Step

Getting Your Documentation
in Order

It is always impressive when a seller and his agent have done their homework prior to listing a home, creating a file of valuable information that includes such items as surveys, warranties, or service contracts to pass on to a buyer. Not only does it make our job as inspectors easier, but it also gives a better presentation for your home, speeds up the sale process, helps remove unknowns that may cause buyer's remorse, and helps to eliminate potentially negative information.

Today, when homes are built, there are reports such as an "As-built" survey, filed at town or city hall, on different components of the house, which would identify the location of the septic system, the well, and the house itself. In addition, there would likely be a well report from the well driller that would give the well recovery information (or how many gallons per minute the well generates). Houses built more than twenty years ago may not have these reports available unless a well was recently drilled or a septic system upgraded. At any rate, if any of this documentation is available, it is good to have it available to the buyer and inspector.

Other helpful information to make available would include:

- original blueprints;
- documentation on additions or upgrades to the home;
- past heating and electric bills;
- information on the alarm system;
- water treatment information; and
- service records on heating and cooling systems.

Information about service contracts for any mechanicals, emergency phone numbers, and warranty information on any appliances is also quite helpful. Documentation for treatment of termites, pests, or vermin is always important to have ready, and you should make it known to your agent or buyers if there are any unique assessments or dues associated with the property.

Prepare a list of improvements, such as when the roof was done, the siding installed, when the water heater was replaced, and so on. It is important to convey any information about past repairs that left evidence behind. Often, when we see evidence such as water stains, it is difficult to determine if they are from an active leak or a past problem that has since been resolved. If you explain this evidence in advance, it gives a feeling of security about the maintenance of your home. Remember, the inspector is going to report on what he or she sees at the time of the inspection and make a judgment about the issue. He is also concerned about giving the client information on potential defects in order to avoid unexpected expenses later. A common discovery in homes is leakage around the chimney flashing, which often leaves permanent water stains on the interior of the chimney. If you have paperwork to document a repair, the buyer and inspector are likely to accept that the stains were from a previous leak and not a current concern.

While you are looking through paperwork, look for warranties on roofing shingles, windows, appliances, the heating system, and termite treatment. These are all a selling advantage, as they will help the buyer determine a reasonable maintenance schedule for the future. If the water heater was just replaced in the past year, it would be fair to assume that there would probably be no expense related to that item for the next five years or more.

It is very important to retain documents that pertain to any removed oil tank, asbestos removal, lead paint abatement, or radon mitigation systems. If there are multiple wells or septic systems, it is important to clarify information pertaining to which ones are being used, and what they serve. You certainly don't want the inspector evaluating the wrong well or septic system, and that has been known to happen. And when a fence is right on or near the property line, you should let your agent or buyer know if it belongs to you, or if it belongs to your neighbor.

Some neighborhoods have associations that influence the choices you have regarding your home. They may have specific requirements for house color, lawn furnishings, or types of roof shingles. If your neighborhood does have these kinds of local standards, have these association rules and regulations available, as well as any information on right-of-way or easements. Be sure to list any association dues or sewer/water assessments to avoid surprises.

If you are selling your home without an agent, it is probably a good idea to get booklets on town or city services, information on parks, beaches, pools, school benefits, and other community information that will highlight the positive aspects of the area. Include information on planned improvements or development that may enhance the quality of life in your community, such as a new park, improvement to roads, a new school or church. Be sure to contact your attorney in advance so that you have the necessary sales agreement forms ready for the sale. If you have decided to have an independent company assist you in your efforts to sell your home, they may provide you with a package of paperwork, but it is still recommended that you consult with your attorney. Having an independent appraisal will also provide a fair sale price for your home. Consider sending a "letter of intent to sell" to your immediate neighbors, as they may have a relative, friend, or associate who may be very interested in the house. Once you have your paperwork together, put it all in a three-ring binder. This professional presentation will impress those who are considering purchasing your home, and will make it easier at the closing. Some people even include pictures taken during construction or renovations of the home, which adds a nice touch.

Though you may not have all of the recommended information available, collect what you do have, put it in a professional format, and you will be sure to impress anyone looking at your home.

After the Home Inspection— Now What?

In this section, I want to touch on how to resolve the problems discovered during the official home inspection—particularly if you don't have a realtor to assist you in preserving the contract. Many buyers today are under the impression that the inspection is a to-do list for the seller. While that may turn out to be true in some cases, it is important to note that you are not required by law to correct most (if any) of the problems discovered during a home inspection prior to conveyance (when the deed is transferred from your name to the buyer's name). The bottom line is that you still own your home. The final decision is yours to make—whether to repair an item, reduce your price to compensate for issues, or stand firm on your price, possibly risking the loss of the sale. There are many factors that will impact your decision, including:

- the fairness of your price in relation to the condition of your home;
- the current market in your area;
- the carrying cost of your home until another buyer arrives;
- your own financial situation; and
- the need to move on to another home.

Paying an attorney for some extra advice may be well worth the cost of a few hundred dollars, as this can be helpful in a private sale and may save you difficulties in the future. It is important that any agreement made between parties be clearly stated and understood by all.

Who Pays for the Termites?

An issue that is commonly negotiated between parties is the presence of termites and termite damage. Most realtors would agree that the cost of treatment by an exterminating company should be borne by the seller, when a contract is based on fair market value. If there is also damage present due to termite activity, I usually recommend that the buyer secure the services of a private building contractor to provide an estimate of repair costs. This is where the resolution can get sticky, as the seller may feel it is his right to repair, while the buyer believes that the quality of the repair should be up to his standards. In addition, the contractor secured by the buyer may inflate the estimate, while the seller may minimize the impact or extent of repairs needed. If this is the

Termite damage on the interior of the home, as shown here
in this oak flooring, could drive a buyer away from a sale.
Repairs should be negotiated between the seller and the
buyer as part of the terms of the contract.

situation you face, consider suggesting that both you and the seller get estimates, and then comparisons can be made. Keep in mind that the contract may need to be extended, as the time needed to get estimates and recommendations for repairs may go beyond the original time line of the contract. If the estimate of the buyer's building contractor seems fair and equitable, it might be advantageous to agree to a price reduction in the range of their estimate. In this way, the repair is out of your hands, leaving the quality or completion of repair to the buyer. When work done by a seller does not meet the expectations of the buyer, the transaction becomes tense, to say the least, and, in the worst-case scenario, may result in the termination of the contract.

Negotiating on the "Handyman's Special"

If you are selling the infamous "handyman's special" at a reduced price, the amount of compensation should be negotiated based on the disclosures you made prior to the sale. If you clearly represented an "as-is" sale, and the price reflected this, compensation may not be warranted, though the sale may still be lost. In any case, once the item has been negotiated, have your attorney review everything in writing.

What to Do When the Buyer Won't Budge

If the requested repairs ultimately rest on your shoulders, it is advised that you retain the services of a professional, licensed, or certified contractor, and check documentation and references. In this way, you can be assured of the professionalism of the work performed, as well as other details such as insurance coverage, standard workmanship, and permit/code requirements in your area. Once you close on the home, you can feel confident that the sale is fully behind you and the work performed will be the responsibility of the professional that you hired. You can always check with the Better Business Bureau (check online at http://www.bbb.org/ for the local office), or other consumer advocacy organizations in your area for reputable contractors. Your state government Web site may have a list of organizations that can help you through their department of consumer protection, or you might check with your local chamber of commerce.

When Tensions Build

It is true that after some seemingly minor findings, realtors and sellers may become agitated. On occasion, I have heard a realtor comment that the inspection is meant to address major concerns, and the minor issues have no place in the process. While on the surface this sounds sensible, the fact of the matter is, a few torn or missing shingles can lead to water penetration that can, in time, cause thousands of dollars' worth of damage to the interior. A defective garage door opener can kill or seriously injure a child. A loose stair tread can cause a fall, and a missing electrical cover can cause shock. If not identified during the inspection process, the buyer would obviously be very upset and likely consider legal action if these items had been overlooked in the inspection. In those states that now have licensing requirements for inspectors, the regulations may clearly spell out the reporting responsibilities of the inspector, as well as ethical considerations. Information on licensing should be available from your state's consumer protection division, either by phone or on the Internet. (In Connecticut, for example, the Web site is http://www.dcp.state.ct.us/licensing/PDFfiles/CPHOI-01.pdf.)

Don't let a few worn roof shingles cause major damage to
your home or jeopardize your sale.

In the end, it may be more equitable for you, the seller, to address the minor repair items prior to the home inspection and sale, hopefully allowing for a smoother transaction. When negotiations are inevitable, try to keep things in perspective by remaining calm and objective. Though you may feel some requests are unfair or petty, if it only amounts to a small percentage of the overall sale price, it may be prudent to agree to repairs or concessions and get on with the sale.

Dealing with Environmental Hazards

We inspectors often hear stories from old-timers reminiscing about how life used to be, extolling the virtues of the olden days before environmental testing. After all, they tell us, all this asbestos, lead, bacteria, and radon was around back then, and they survived!

There may be a few people who feel that home inspections and environmental testing are just more ways of taking money from consumers, but if you had a contract on a house, and the inspection process uncovered a leaking, underground oil tank, you would likely question the merits of the "good old days." The cost of a mandatory cleanup of such an oil spill is astronomical, not to mention the additional expense if the well water had been contaminated by the oil spill. These negative comments from some sellers often result from their displeasure at having been negatively impacted by the tests and inspections. Certainly, the real estate agents work very hard to keep contracts intact when negative findings are revealed. But the buyer is entitled to a clear understanding and full disclosure of all the components of the purchase. While there are those who are unaffected by lead paint or asbestos, those families who have suffered from exposure to hazardous materials would agree that awareness is our best ally. If nothing else, buyers have a right to know all they can about their purchase, and it is their prerogative to request specific testing.

Who Should I Hire?

It can be very confusing to know who to hire when work needs to be done on your home. We refer to the need for experts, but some people go by titles that are contradictory and confusing. Here are some general guidelines to Who's Who in the Field:

- **Builder**—This term is often interchangeable with contractor and carpenter. A builder might be a contractor, or might be sort of a one-man company, who is capable of doing many of the tasks on a given job, except for those that need licensed people (electrician, plumber, etc). A builder might do everything from the framing to the roofing to the interior sheetrock.

- **Carpenter**—A carpenter is usually hired by a builder to work together with a team of carpenters. He could also be an individual who does a variety of tasks, such as installing shelves, repairing sheetrock, or adding on a deck. We usually think of a carpenter as one who would be utilized for the smaller jobs that don't require special certification (such as a plumber, electrician, etc.).

- **Contractor**—A contractor may or may not have firsthand building experience. A contractor is usually the person or entity that hires the electricians, plumbers, roofers, and other specialists to complete a building project. Contractors will usually hire subcontractors who specialize in specific areas, such as plumbing, electrical, roofing, or sheetrocking. This is helpful if there is a big project to be done, and you want one person to oversee the entire job.

- **Engineer**—An engineer is a specialist with a degree in a specific field of engineering. Most often, the building field utilizes a structural engineer, who is a specialist in determining how the structure of a building should be designed. A structural engineer would also be called in when unusual movement in the home is noted, and this specialist would research the cause, suggesting methods to alleviate the problem.

- **Licensed Electrician**—One who has passed the required coursework, testing, and apprentice work to become licensed in a given state. A licensed electrician can apply for permits for specific electrical work on a structure.

- **Licensed Plumber**—One who has passed the required coursework, testing, and apprentice work to become licensed in a given state. A licensed plumber can apply for permits for specific plumbing work on a structure. Many plumbers are also licensed to install some heating systems, as they require installation of water pipes.

Home Seller's Preparation Checklist

This checklist is designed to be your partner to the walkthrough inspection outlined in parts 1 through 4 of this book. Make a copy of it to have on hand as you go through your inspection. When you discover something that needs attention, check it off and make some notes about any products or tools you might need. You might want to do the inspection in sections, rather than all at one time, as the complete inspection could take up to two or three hours. Once completed, you will have a good idea about the task ahead of you. It will also give you information that will be helpful in deciding when to list your house (if your list is long, you may want to do some of the work before listing) or how to price your home (if your home is in need of more than you can do on your own, maybe your price will reflect that fact).

The Outdoors

Exterior

Look at home from the outside

Paint needed

Wood rot on exterior, especially:

❏ Garage door trim

❏ Corner boards

❏ Fascia

❏ Deck supports/joists

Vinyl siding—check for:

❏ Loose siding

❏ Damaged siding

Windows—check for:

❏ Broken, cracked panes

❏ Glazing on single-pane windows

❏ Condition of storm units

❏ Broken seal or fogging of Thermopane windows (double-pane)

❏ Condition of sills

❏ Condition of casings

Steps:

❏ Loose treads

❏ Rotted wood

❏ Spalling cement (deterioration of surface)

❏ Railings—are they needed, and are they secure?

❏ Spaces between railings—are they close enough to prevent a child from falling through, particularly on a deck?

Exterior doors:

❏ Finish of doors

❏ Weather stripping

❏ Rotted areas

Sliders:

❏ Operation—need lubricant?

❏ Clear or fogged?

❏ Screen—operation, condition

❏ Condition of hardware

Electrical:

❏ GFI outlets—test and reset

❏ Entry wire—worn or damaged?

❏ Entry wire—secure?

Notes on Exterior Needs:

_____

_____

_____

_____

_____

_____

Landscaping

Shrubs—how close to house?

Shrubs—trimming needed?

Tree limbs—overhanging too close to home?

Growth on house—vines, etc.

Driveway:

❏ Cracks

❏ Transitions: driveway to garage and driveway to road

❏ Parking—tight or generous?

Fencing:

❏ Wood, metal, or vinyl?

❏ Condition

❏ Replacement boards needed?

Grading—slope of land:

❏ Toward house

❏ Away from house

Wood/soil contact

Mud tubes (termites)?

Evidence of carpenter ants or bees?

Walkways:

❏ Cracks

❏ Raised surfaces/trip hazards

❏ General deterioration

Notes on Landscaping Needs:

_____

_____

_____

_____

_____

_____

Roof and Chimneys

Age of roof

Pitch of roof (very steep, steep, flat?)

Number of layers

Asphalt shingle condition:

❏ Brittle

❏ Cracked

❏ Curled

❏ Loss of mineral surface

❏ Lifted or missing shingles

Wood shingle condition:

❏ Warped

❏ Moss-covered

❏ Cracked

❏ Percentage of damaged shingles

Tile roof condition:

❏ Cracks

❏ Missing

❏ Broken

Chimneys:

❏ Brick/metal/block

❏ Lining—tile?

❏ Metal—insulated?

❏ Condition of flashing—loose, missing?

❏ Cement in chimney—repointing needed?

❏ Cracks

❏ Secure to house

❏ Spalling—deterioration of surface

❏ Crown condition

❏ Exterior surface of chimney from attic

Notes on Roof/Chimney Needs:

_____

_____

_____

_____

_____

_____

Garage

Fire Protection:

❏ Common walls—⅝-inch drywall w/tape

❏ Fire-rated door

❏ Floor of garage below level of home floor

Automatic garage door opener:

❏ Safety reverse feature working properly

❏ Dedicated outlet

Manually operated:

❏ Smooth operation

❏ Opens/closes at reasonable pace—doesn't slam

❏ Springs—adjustment/lubrication

Finish

Gasket of door

Wood

Metal door (dents)

Electrical:

❏ Hanging wires

❏ Open splices

❏ Open junction boxes

❏ Abandoned wires

Plumbing:

❏ Adequate heat source

Windows

Stairs:

❏ Treads

❏ Railing

Floor:

❏ Cracks

❏ Gas spills

Structural:

❏ Framing near garage door

❏ Board or plate touching floor for rot

Notes on Garage Needs:

The Indoors

Basement/Crawl Space

Access door—condition of access area:

❏ Vermin- and weatherproof

❏ Easy to open/close

Debris at access area or inside?

Ventilation:

❏ Vent screens/windows

❏ Moisture

Joists:
- ❏ Soft
- ❏ Rotten

Insulation:
- ❏ Fallen
- ❏ Loose
- ❏ Paper side toward living space

Mud tubes—termites

Floor:
- ❏ Condition
- ❏ Dirt floor covered with plastic

Window condition:
- ❏ Frames
- ❏ Glass panes

Voids or light coming through foundation walls

Look for evidence of vermin/animals (feces)

Heat source (northern climates, to prevent pipes freezing)

Condition of wiring in crawl space:
- ❏ Open splices
- ❏ Loose wiring
- ❏ BX cable condition

Metal support columns—rusty?

Check running water in supply or drainpipes

Beam supports:
- ❏ Settled
- ❏ Rotted
- ❏ Fallen over

Ductwork:
- ❏ Damaged
- ❏ Rusty
- ❏ Disconnected

Lighting:
- ❏ Easy to turn on from access
- ❏ Lightbulbs working

Notes on Basement/Crawl Space Needs:

_____

_____

_____

_____

_____

_____

_____

Attic

Clean out closet or area where hatch is located

Move stored boxes/items from attic walkway (stay on decked area only)

Secure loose boards

Roof vents clear

Replace lightbulb if needed

Rearrange loose/missing insulation

Vents to exterior

Adequate ventilation—clear areas:

❏ Gable vents

❏ Ridge vents

❏ Soffit vents

❏ Attic fan

Roof sheathing:

❏ Dry

❏ Mold/mildew

Wiring:

❏ Open splices

❏ Open junction boxes

❏ Frayed/hanging wires

Rafters/trusses:

❏ Cracked

❏ Broken

Exterior light showing

Leaks:

❏ Chimney

❏ Roof

Hatch cover

Pull-down stairs

Notes on Attic Needs:

_____

_____

_____

_____

_____

_____

Fireplaces and Woodstoves

Chimney cleaned

Clean firebox

Check damper:

❏ Rusty

❏ Loose

Hearth secure

Broken bricks

Loose grout

Doors—operational

No fires just before or during inspection

Firewood storage in good place

Woodstove—space of 18 inches to combustible surface

Consult with fire marshal for more information

Notes on Fireplace Needs:

_____

_____

_____

_____

_____

_____

Laundry Room

Vent pipe:

❏ Plastic or metal?

❏ Vented to exterior of home

❏ Exterior of vent cover intact and unclogged

Service connections to dryer secure

Washer plumbing:

❏ Supply valves leak-free

❏ Corrosion

❏ Discharge pipe intact

❏ Discharges to adequate system

❏ Laundry sink drain

Light fixture

Clean area of dirty or smelly clothes

Notes on Laundry Needs:

_____

_____

_____

_____

_____

_____

Bathrooms

Floor:

❏ Cracked tiles

❏ Loose/cracking grout

❏ Peeling/torn vinyl

❏ Spongy areas near tub or toilet

❏ Caulk around tub area

Vanity:

❏ Leaks

❏ Corrosion on pipes/faucet

❏ Surface of sink

❏ Surface of counter

GFI outlet

Toilet:

❏ Stains

❏ Cracks

❏ Flush

Venting:

❏ Window

❏ Fan—clean, vented to exterior

Walls

Ceiling

Tub/shower enclosure:

❏ Loose/cracked tiles

❏ Joint between wall/tub caulked

❏ Clean

❏ Drains freely

❏ Leaky faucet

❏ Shower door—clean tracks

Notes on Bathroom Space Needs:

_____

_____

_____

_____

_____

_____

Interior

Kitchen:

❏ Clean cabinets

❏ Cabinets/drawers operational

❏ Clear counters

❏ Stove—elements working

❏ Check ventilator—fan and bulb

❏ Dishwasher—door springs intact

❏ Dishwasher—drains properly

Finishes of walls/ceilings:

❏ Stains

❏ Cracks

❏ Paint

Floors:

❏ Carpet cleaned

❏ Wood floors buffed or refinished

❏ Tile floors—cracks or loose grout

Windows:

❏ Open/close easily

❏ Hardware intact

❏ Clean glass

❏ Handles intact on casements

❏ Fogging on Thermopane windows

❏ Screens

Interior doors:

❏ Even gaps on all sides of doors when closed

❏ Evidence of settling

❏ Damaged doors

❏ Hardware intact

❏ Bifold doors

Stairs:

❏ Railings present and secure

❏ Openings small enough

❏ Stair treads

❏ Stair safety

Interior electrical:

❏ Cover plates on outlets and switches

❏ Light fixtures throughout interior are working

❏ Loose/missing fixtures

❏ Loose outlets

Clear access areas

Remove stored cars in garage

Empty wastebaskets on day of inspection

Note unusual items for inspector

Prepare home for weather of day of inspection:

❏ Shovel snow

❏ Heat home on cold days

❏ Cool house on hot days if you have air conditioning

❏ Make home comfortable and palatable to your buyer

Notes on Interior Needs:

_____

_____

_____

_____

_____

_____

The Utilities

Heating

Heating fuel—oil, gas, or electric

Delivery of heat—ductwork, baseboard, radiant

Age of heating unit

Operation of system:

❑ Shut-off switches on

❑ Service tags on unit

❑ No debris near unit

❑ Serviced within past twelve months?

❑ Warm air—change filter

❑ Warm air—voids or rusted areas

❑ Water, hydronic system—leaks

❑ Flue pipe—rusted or open areas

Zones—operate all areas

Thermostats in good condition:

❑ Comfortable temperature on day of inspection

❑ Condition of baseboards

❑ Presence of asbestos on heating pipes

Location of fuel tank:

❑ Underground (documentation of removed tank?)

Location of fuel lines:

❑ Going through concrete?

❑ Inside conduit

Rusty radiators

Loose valves

Loose/damaged baseboards

Notes on Heating Needs:

_____

_____

_____

_____

_____

_____

Plumbing

Kitchen faucet:

- ❏ Leaky at base (swing arm of faucet back and forth)
- ❏ Dripping
- ❏ Trap under sink
- ❏ Feed pipes under sink
- ❏ Base of cabinet for evidence of leakage

Bath faucets:

- ❏ Leaky at base
- ❏ Dripping
- ❏ Trap under sink
- ❏ Feed pipes under sink
- ❏ Base of cabinet for evidence of leakage
- ❏ Drain plug

Tub faucet:

- ❏ Leaky around valve or faucet
- ❏ Shower diverter
- ❏ Drain plug

Toilets:

- ❏ Flush runs on
- ❏ Flush not adequate
- ❏ Leaky around base
- ❏ Cracks or broken seat

Water filters:

- ❏ Change any water filters
- ❏ Environmental water testing

Basement supply pipes

Vent pipe to exterior (above roof)

Leaks in crawl/basement

Water heater:

- ❏ Puddling
- ❏ Rust spots
- ❏ Relief valve extending to 6 to 10 inches above ground
- ❏ Adequate hot water
- ❏ Flue pipe condition
- ❏ Move stored items away from water heater
- ❏ Expansion tank—hollow sound
- ❏ Water pressure—slight drop when two or more fixtures running at one time
- ❏ Water treatment systems serviced
- ❏ Documentation on water systems

Well:

❑ Cap/concrete lid secure

❑ Openings where rodents can enter

❑ Hazardous materials stored near well should be moved

Notes on Plumbing Needs:

_____

_____

_____

_____

_____

_____

Electrical

Load center:

❑ Openings visible from outside

❑ Cover missing

❑ Fuse style

❑ Breaker style

❑ Size of service if known (main breaker)

Main entry wire:

❑ Damaged

❑ Worn sheathing

❑ Loose

GFI outlets:

❑ Bathrooms

❑ Kitchens

❑ Exterior

❑ Pool / hot tub

Older wiring:

❑ Knob and tube wiring

❑ BX wiring (armored cable)—rusty, corroded?

❑ Aluminum wiring

Other defects to be checked by electrician

Smoke detectors

Notes on Electrical Needs:

_____

_____

_____

_____

_____

Environmental Hazards

Environmental Concerns

Radon in air

Radon in water

Presence of asbestos

Presence of mold/mildew

Lead in water (common for FHA mortgages)

Lead in paint

Air quality

Soil contamination

Other water tests

Notes on Environmental Needs:

_____

_____

_____

_____

_____

A Time to Make Decisions

Now that you have your completed list, look it over and prioritize what to address first. If your list is very long, you might want to address the most glaring issues prior to listing your home with a realtor. You could set up a meeting with your realtor to discuss your options, and decide on a time frame for completing your list and getting your home on the market.

Approximate Repair /
Improvement Costs

There are so many factors that affect the pricing of improvements and repairs that it is difficult to cover them all. As a general rule, though, if you live in a region of the U.S. that is at the high end of the housing market (such as New England or California), you can expect the contractor prices to be at the high end of the range outlined here. If you live in an area where costs are much lower (such as North Carolina or Mississippi), it is likely that the labor costs will reflect this trend. Costs for materials can also vary, though not quite as significantly.

Another consideration to keep in mind is that a high hourly rate does not always mean that the job will cost you more. A highly skilled contractor with the proper equipment can usually perform a task in a shorter amount of time, and with greater professionalism than the handyman who is a jack-of-all-trades. Contractors, builders, and carpenters may charge by the hour or by the job. Specialists such as electricians, plumbers, engineers, and masons will often charge more than a carpenter, as they have pursued specialized training and certification. These details should be worked out in advance, and if paying by the hour, a qualified tradesman should be able to give you an estimate of the time involved. If you are not familiar with any local contractors, be sure to get several bids, check for licensing and insurance, and ask for references—and then be sure to take the time to follow up on those references.

It is recommended that a budget of roughly 1 percent of the value of the home be set aside annually to cover unexpected repairs and annual maintenance.

These approximate costs are estimates based on a typical three-bedroom ranch and are not intended to represent or influence, in any way, the value of a property.

Structural

Structural Improvements ....$60 per hr. and up
Foundation Improvements ....$60 per hr. and up
Floor Structure Improvements...............................$60 per hr. and up
Wall Structure Improvements ....$60 per hr. and up

Roof Structure Improvements...$60 per hr. and up
Termite (subterranean) Chemical Treatment.......................$600 to 1,500
Termite (subterranean) Baiting Treatment..........................$600 to 1,500
Carpenter Ant Treatment..$200 to 400
Carpenter Bee Treatment ....$150 to 400
Lot Drainage Improvements..$500 and up
Foundation Crack Repairs...$400 to 800
(depending on approach)

Roofing

Sloped Roofing Replacement..$3,500 to 5,500
(removal of layers adds to cost)
Sloped Roofing Repairs..$200 and up
Flat Roofing Replacement..$1,000 to 2,000
(for approx. 20-by-20-foot area)
Flat Roofing Improvements ....$35 to 75 hourly
Porch Roofing Improvements ....$1,000 to 1,500
Flashing Improvements..$35 to 75 hourly
Skylight Improvements..$35 to 75 hourly
Chimney Improvements...$45 to 75 hourly
Gutter and Downspout Improvements ....$100 to 300
Gutter and Downspout Replacement...............................$700 to 1,500

Exterior

Paint/Stain Exterior Wall Surfaces and Trim ....$1,000 and up
Paint/Caulk Windows and Trim.......................................$500 and up
Siding Repairs and Painting...$1,500 and up
Siding Replacement...$3,500 to 7,500
Exterior Wall Cleaning..$250 and up
Window Replacement...$350 and up (each)
Storm Window Installation ....$75 to 150 each
Install Aluminum Soffit/Fascia and Gutters ....$1,200 to 2,000
Lot Drainage Improvements..$500 and up
Overhead Garage Door Repairs..$200 and up
Overhead Garage Door Replacement ....$700 to 1,200
Install Overhead Garage Door Opener.............................$200 to 400
Rebuild Garage...$5,000 and up

Driveway Drain Improvements..$300 to 800
Resurface Driveway (asphalt installation)............................$1,500 to 5,000
Driveway Surface Sealant ....$200 to 1,000
Deck Improvements..$250 and up
Build Deck ....$13 per sq. ft. and up
Tree Trimming (per tree)..$250 to 350
Tree Removal (per tree)..$300 to 1,000

Electrical

Upgrade Electrical Service to 100 Amps ....$1,000 to 1,700
Upgrade Electrical Service to 200 Amps ....$1,400 to 2,500
Electrical Service Entrance Repairs....................................$500 to 1,000
Electrical Panel Improvements ....$60 per hr. and up
Replace Main Electrical Panel ....$500 to 800
Distribution Wire Improvements ....$60 per hr. and up
Aluminum Wire Improvements ....$500 and up
Add Additional Electrical Outlets......................................$60 and up (each)
Add GFCI Receptacles/Breakers ....$60 and up (each)
Add 220V Dedicated Electrical Circuit ....$150 to 350

Heating

Boiler Replacement ....$3,500 and up
Furnace Replacement...$3,500 and up
High-Efficiency Furnace...$3,000 to 5,000
Furnace Repairs..$200 and up
Humidifier Repairs ....$60 to 150
Ductwork Cleaning ....$150 to 400
Ductwork Improvements ....$60 per hr. and up
Boiler Replacement ....$3,000 to 5,000
Boiler Repairs...$200 and up
Add Circulating Pump to Heating System ....$300 to 500
Radiator Control Valve Repairs...$60 each (approx.)
Chimney Liner Installation...$500 to 1,500
Oil Tank Removal ....$150 and up
Buried Oil Tank Removal (intact) ....$2,500 and up
Electric Heater Repairs..$60 per hr. and up
Electric Baseboard Heater Installation ....$150 and up (each)

Set-Back Thermostat Installation ....$75 to 150
Central Air Conditioning Installation (w/out ductwork) ....$2,500 to 3,500
Heat Pump Installation ....$3,000 to 4,000
Independent Air Conditioning Installation (inc. ductwork) ...$5,000 and up

Cooling / Heat Pump

Air Conditioning System Replacement.............................$2,000 to 3,000
  (compressor and air handler)
Heat Pump Replacement ....$3,000 to 5,000
Cooling System Compressor Replacement ....$800 to 1,200
Air Conditioning Improvements ....$60 per hr. and up
Heat Pump Improvements ....$60 per hr. and up
Ductwork Cleaning ....$150 to 400
Electronic Air Cleaner Installation...................................$400 to 600
Ductwork Improvements ....$60 per hr. and up
Set-Back Thermostat Installation ....$75 to 150

Insulation / Ventilation

Insulation Improvements ....$60 per hr. and up
Attic Insulation Improvements ....$1,000 to 2,000
Ventilation Improvements ....$60 per hr. and up
Attic Ventilation Improvements ....$200 to 500
Roof Ventilation Improvements.......................................$200 to 600
Basement Insulation Improvements ....$60 per hr. and up
Crawl Space Insulation Improvements..............................$60 per hr. and up
Crawl Space Ventilation Improvements.............................$200 to 700
Moisture Barrier Installation in Crawl Space (plastic) ....$150 to 250
Vermin Prevention Measures...$150 to 600

Plumbing

Water Heater Replacement (higher for gas or oil units) .....$600 to 1,200
Water Heater Improvements...$100 to 300
Gas Piping Improvements ....$60 per hr. and up
Supply Piping Improvements...$60 per hr. and up
Replace Water Pump ....$300 to 1,500

Waste Piping Improvements ....$60 per hr. and up
Faucet Replacement ....$100 and up (each)
Bathtub Enclosure Repairs...$50 and up
Bathtub Enclosure Rebuilding ....$500 to 1,000
Whirlpool Bath Repairs..$60 per hr. and up
Shower Stall Repairs ....$50 and up
Shower Stall Rebuilding ....$1,500 to 2,500
Toilet Replacement..$200 and up
Toilet Seal Replacement ....$100 to 200
Sink Replacement..$150 and up
Laundry Tubs/Sink Replacement ....$150 to 400
Exhaust Fan Installation ....$200 to 500
Sump Pump Repairs...$60 to 150
Sump Pump Replacement ....$150 to 300
Waste Ejector Pump Repairs...$60 to 250
Waste Ejector Pump Replacement ....$300 to 500
Laundry Pump Replacement ....$150 to 300
Septic Tank Replacement..$1,500 to 3,000
Leaching Field Improvements..$350 to 2,000 and up
Installation of Riser for Septic Tank Access........................$150 to 250
Water Softening Equipment Installation ....$800 to 2,500
Ultraviolet Equipment Installation....................................$700 to 2,000
Complete Bathroom Renovation ....$2,500 and up

Interior

Wall and Ceiling Repairs ....$60 per hr. and up
Floor Repairs..$60 per hr. and up
Tile Floor Improvements ....$60 per hr. and up
Vinyl Floor Improvements ....$60 per hr. and up
Sanding/Refinishing Hardwood Floors ....$250 to 800 per room
Window Improvements..$60 per hr. and up
Door Improvements...$60 per hr. and up
Door and Window Improvements ....$60 per hr. and up
Windows Replacement...$250 to 375 per unit
Counter Improvements..$60 per hr. and up
Cabinet Improvements ....$60 per hr. and up
Skylight Repairs..$200 and up
Handrail Installation ....$100 to 300

Railing Installation..$500 and up
Stairway Improvements ....$60 per hr. and up
Chimney Cleaning..$150 to 500
Fireplace Repairs ....$60 per hr. and up
Hearth Improvements ....$60 per hr. and up
Woodstove Repairs ....$60 per hr. and up
Basement Leakage Improvements.......................................$300 and up

Appliances

Appliance Repairs..$60 and up
Range Repairs..$60 and up
Oven Repairs ....$60 and up
Cooktop Repairs ....$60 and up
Microwave Repairs ....$60 and up
Dishwasher Repairs..$60 and up
Waste Disposer Repairs..$60 and up
Trash Compactor Repairs ....$60 and up
Refrigerator Repairs ....$60 and up
Freezer Repairs ....$60 and up
Clothes Washer Repairs..$100 and up
Clothes Dryer Repairs ....$100 and up
Exhaust Fan Repairs ....$60 and up
Central Vacuum Repairs...$100 and up
Doorbell Repairs ....$60 and up
Intercom Repairs ....$100 and up
Smoke Detector Improvements ....$60 and up
Instant Hot Water Dispenser Repairs.................................$60 and up
Water Conditioning Equipment Repairs.............................$100 and up

Environmental

Radon in Air Testing...$80 to 150
Radon in Air Mitigation System ....$900 to 1,500
Radon in Water Testing...$80 to 125
Radon in Water Mitigation System ....$3,000 to 5,000
Asbestos Testing (lab)..$45 and up
Asbestos Removal ....$500 to 5,000 and up

Lead Paint Testing ....$300 to 700

Lead Paint Removal...$500 to 5,000 and up

Mold in Air Testing..$300 and up

Mold Mitigation ....$100 to 1,000 and up
(depending upon
severity)

Oil or Chemical Spills...$1,000 to 10,000 and up

Glossary of Inspection Terms

While some people are familiar with all the technical terms of a house, many people are very confused by the language, so it is important to understand the correct terminology. Here is a list of typical words and phrases used in home inspection reports.

ABS piping (Acrylonitrile Butadiene Styrene Pipe)—Usually the thick black plastic waste piping.

Air handler—A fan or blower assembly used to force either cold or warm air through a ducting system. It usually has an exchanger mounted within it that has either a hot or cool fluid circulating within it, and a fan blowing across the hot or cool piping.

Asbestos cement shingles—These are older shingles that were used as siding material. Proper precautions must be used when removing or disturbing asbestos shingles. Sometimes, when removing aluminum or vinyl siding, you may uncover old, asbestos shingles. If you are unsure as to whether or not you have asbestos shingles, contact an asbestos removal company or testing company before disturbing the siding.

Attic decking—These are the boards or sheets of plywood placed on top of ceiling joists to create a walking surface or storage area in an attic.

Awning windows—A window sash that opens on hinges at the top.

Bay windows—A window or series of windows forming a bay in a room and projecting outward from the wall.

Boiler—A generator of hot water or steam that is fueled by liquid, gas, or solid fuel. Examples are oil, natural gas, propane, wood, etc. The heat from a boiler is usually distributed through pipes, either water or steam. The hot water or steam is piped to baseboards, radiant heaters in ceilings, walls and floors, or through radiators.

Bow window—Usually a curved bay window.

Built-up beams—These are traditional-sized pieces of lumber nailed together to make up a thicker beam, such as three 2-by-6-inch studs nailed together to make a 6-by-6-inch beam.

Burner—The source of heat mounted either on a boiler or furnace. Usually it is activated by liquid fuel and has a built-in ignition to create the heat.

BX wires—Armored, metal-covered, distribution electrical wiring. This brings the electricity from the load center to the individual outlets or fixtures.

Casement windows—A window sash that opens on hinges at the side.

Casing—The border trim around a window or door.

Ceiling joists—These are the framing members in the attic that hold up the ceiling of the rooms below.

Circulating pump—A pump that is usually installed on water systems to deliver heat to a specific area or zone.

Clad units—Usually a vinyl or aluminum veneer applied to the exterior of the window.

Clapboards—These are horizontal lengths of beveled wood boards that are used for siding.

Collar ties—Crosspieces of framing that help keep the rafters from spreading.

Combustion chamber—The area that captures the heat from a burner; usually has some form of fireproofing to direct the heat to some form of an exchanger (water or air).

Condensate pump—An electric pump on an air conditioning unit that is designed to remove liquid condensate (water) as the air is cooled.

Conductors—The composition of the inner metal or conductor, which is usually copper or aluminum.

Damper—A hinged flap that can be opened or closed; may be used in a flue or in ductwork.

Doorjamb—An upright piece forming the side of a door opening.

Double-hung window—A window unit with two moveable sashes that raise and lower to allow ventilation.

Downspout extensions—Extension pipes installed at the end of gutter downspouts to carry the water away from the foundation of the home.

Drivit (or Dryvit)—A manufactured stucco siding material that has been known to have some problems with the connection joints.

Drywall—Wallboard made into sheet stock, usually taped to a smooth finish (sheetrock).

Electrical defects (outlet defects)—Reverse polarity, ungrounded, open ground outlets. These are items that can be detected with an electrical tester and require further evaluation by an electrician.

Electrical defects (wire connections)—Open splices, junction boxes without cover plates, abandoned wires; items for further evaluation by an electrician.

Expansion tank—A hollow tank that may have a rubber bladder in it to absorb water as it is heated and expands.

Fabric-covered wires—An older wiring with a cloth or fabric insulative outer covering on the wires. In most cases, this old wiring should be replaced.

Fascia boards—These boards are located behind the gutters, and cover the rafter ends.

Fiberglass batts—An insulating material used in exterior walls, ceiling joists, and above the basement floor to reduce heating and cooling costs.

Firebox—The containment or structure around a fire, usually made of masonry or steel.

Fire doors—Doors specifically manufactured for divider walls between garage and living space, or for commercial applications where it is important to slow a fire, giving occupants more time to vacate the structure.

Flex ducting—Flexible ducting material used in heating or cooling air systems to channel the air to specific rooms. It usually has a plastic interior with fiberglass outer coating, encapsulated in another plastic coating.

Floor joists—These are structural framing members that form the framing of the floor.

Floor trusses—These are flooring sections that are prefabricated at a factory to carry a floor load, and usually take the place of floor joists.

Flue—An enclosed passageway for directing a current of gas or smoke. It may be a single wall flue, tile lined, unlined, PVC, or insulated pipe, depending on the application or age of the chimney/flue.

Fogged glass—A condition that is caused by air infiltration in the space between the panes of glass in a Thermopane unit. This allows moisture sediment to adhere to the glass and causes a clouding effect over time.

Footing—The concrete support poured below the foundation wall (below the grade and rarely visible).

Foundation—The support wall below the walls of the house proper.

Friable—When a material, such as asbestos, can be crumbled to a powder by your hand (which of course you should never do yourself, as it would release harmful particles into the air).

Furnace—A generator of heat that is fueled by liquid, gas, or solid fuel. Examples would be oil, natural gas, propane, wood, etc. A furnace heats the air and has a fan or blower that supplies warm air through a ducting system.

Gable—A roofline that looks like a triangle.

Gable vents—These are vents, either screened or louvered, that are mounted at the gable ends of the attic space, just below the roofline, allowing ventilation in the attic.

GFCI (Ground Fault Circuit Interrupter)—A type of safety outlet, commonly installed in wet locations such as kitchens, baths, exterior outlets, pools, etc. The outlet is designed to "trip," or shut down, if there is a sudden surge of electricity, which would keep the consumer safe from electrocution.

Grading—The level and angle of the ground around the perimeter of the home.

Ground wire—The main wire that bonds to either an exterior rod driven in the ground, or a wire strapped to a copper water pipe, or both.

Headers—These are structural members that help bridge loads over windows, doors, or other openings.

Hollow-core doors—Thin veneers made into a sandwich with some form of spacers within to provide rigidity.

Hopper windows—A window sash that opens on hinges at the bottom, and opens into the room.

Humidifier—A device that injects water or steam to the warm air of a furnace, increasing the humidity level for a better comfort level. It is usually mounted on the side of a furnace plenum, which is the sheet-metal air distribution box where the ductwork originates.

Indirect, or "side arm" water heater—An insulated tank that is separate from the boiler, supplying domestic hot water, with some form of hot water transfer with an exchanger. Usually an external pump circulates hot water through it. This is often done to increase the amount of hot water to meet demand.

Insulation—A material placed in ceiling, wall, floor, or rafter cavities to help hold in heat or keep the home cool in warmer temperatures.

Jalousie window—A window made of adjustable glass louvers that control ventilation.

Joist—Ceiling or floor supports in building construction that are laid in a parallel series across the length of the structure.

Kick board—A sturdy panel, usually made of metal, that is added to the lower portion of a door to protect it from kicking.

Knob and tube wiring—Very old, obsolete wiring with porcelain separators.

Lally columns—Posts (usually made of steel) that are filled with concrete and used as supports.

Laminated beams—These are sections of wood plys, or composite materials, bonded together with glues or resins.

Leaders—Piping that is attached to gutters to direct water down or to other locations, such as another gutter at a lower level.

Lintels—Usually metal or masonry lengths that help bridge loads over masonry openings such as fireplaces, windows, doors, etc.

Load-bearing walls—These are support walls or structural, bearing walls that are important to maintaining adequate support to floors, roof, etc.

Load center—The main electrical panel box that houses circuit breakers (or fuses) and the distribution center.

Metal ducting—Rigid metal housing to channel cool or warm air to a specific room. It can have insulation applied to exterior (some even have insulation on the interior).

Newel post—The larger vertical post supporting a stair rail.

Oriented Strand Board (OSB)—A product used for sheathing that was formed through pressing wood chips at high pressure with various resins creating sheet stock. The strands are oriented in a specific direction, not randomly placed.

Partitions—These are walls that divide a space, but are not necessarily important to holding up floors, roofs, etc.

pH system—A system used to adjust the pH level of water to maintain it within an acceptable level, which is considered to be between 6.4 and 10.0. Low pH in water is common in certain areas, and results in acidic water that may cause corrosion on pipes and fixtures.

Piers—Support posts, which can be masonry, wood, steel, or concrete.

Plaster—Typical material of older walls that was hand-troweled over wood laths, forming a smooth wall finish when dried.

Plywood—A sheathing material that is formed through bonding wood veneers together at opposing grain directions to form a large sheet.

Polyvinyl Chloride Pipe (PVC)—A strong, durable plastic material used in either supply or waste pipes; usually the white piping used in plumbing.

Rafters—Framing members, typically wood, that hold the roofline in place.

Raised panel doors—Doors with a multilevel surface; can be solid wood panels, or hollow, molded units.

Rake boards—These run along the gable, covering the end rafters. They can be seen when looking up at the exterior.

Relief valve—A safety valve that is preset to release excessive pressure and is usually installed on boilers or water heaters.

Repointing—The process of filling loose or open masonry joints, sometimes referred to as grouting.

Return piping or return ducting—This is the return of either the air or water to the unit for reheating or recooling.

Ridge—The peak of the roof, running horizontally.

Ridge vents—These are vents that are cut into the peak of a roof, allowing air flow in the attic space.

Rim joist—The end joist that runs perpendicular to a series of joists.

Risers—This is the front face of the stair, or the vertical piece between the stringers and below each tread.

Rock wool—An early manufactured insulation product.

Romex wires—Plastic-coated distribution wiring used today.

Roof trusses—These are roof sections that are engineered specifically for the designed home, and prefabricated at a factory, used instead of rafters.

Roof vents—These are usually individual vents that mount on the surface of the roof to provide attic ventilation.

Rotary valves—Valves with round handles to turn water on or off.

Sash—The framework in which panes of glass are set in a window.

Sediment filter—A filtration system used to remove particles in water such as rust, sand, debris, and some minerals.

Service entry wire—The main wire that delivers the power from the pole to the house.

Sheathing—Typically made of plywood, but may also be planks installed over the rafters, trusses, or walls to give an exterior skin to the home.

Shingles—Exterior, waterproof covering to keep the home dry. Shingles could be asphalt or wood for the roof, or wood for the siding. Shingles used as siding are short pieces placed side by side, unlike long lengths of clapboard.

Sistering—Adding another framing member to the side of a compromised member (one that is notched, cracked, or termite-damaged, etc.)

Skirt board—The lowest horizontal board at the base of the exterior.

Sliding window—A window unit that has one or more sashes that glide sideways within a track.

Soffits—The exterior underside of the lower edge of the roof, where the rafter ends. These are usually perpendicular to the fascia boards. Soffit ventilation is often located here in homes built today.

Softener—Tanks containing minerals or ion-exchange resins, which contain sodium ions that change places with the calcium and magnesium.

Solid beams—These are large wood members, such as 4-by-4-inch, or 6-by-6-inch, or even 8-by-8-inch (in various lengths), used for support. The larger the beam, the greater the strength.

Spalling—Surface deterioration of masonry surface.

Spindles and balusters—Interior lengths of a material that help close in the rail openings between the rail and the treads or floor.

Splash blocks—Preformed masonry or plastic water diverters placed at the base of a downspout.

Steel I-beams—Steel beams that are formed in the shape of an I.

Strike plate—The metal plate that the strike, or bolt, latches into, mounted on the doorjamb.

Stringers—These are the two stairway supports that run lengthwise on the side of the stairs. The stair treads are placed between the two stringers.

Studs—These are the framing members that make up the outer walls, usually 2-by-6-inch, or even 2-by-8-inch.

Subflooring—This is the sheathing applied directly to floor joists. In many cases, finished flooring is applied on top of this material.

Supply piping or supply ductwork—This is the outgoing air or water in a heating or air conditioning system. Also refers to pipes used to supply domestic water to and within a building. Supply water piping is made of copper, galvanized steel, PVC, Pex, or other plastics. In the past, lead piping was used, which caused lead poisoning, as the lead leached into the water itself. If a home has lead supply piping, it is necessary to update it to acceptable supply piping material.

Tankless heater—Usually mounted in a boiler to supply domestic water on demand to a dwelling.

TGI-engineered lumber—A technique that uses heat and pressure to bond high-grade wood fiber together to form virtually defect-free lumber capable of supporting heavy loads. It is usually shaped like steel I-beams.

Thermopane windows/doors—Bonded glass panes that form a double pane and create an insulated glass insert.

Thermostat—The wall-mounted sensor that commands the heating or cooling source to engage or disengage. Some have programmable features (or switches mounted on them) that change the mode from heating to cooling.

Threshold—The plank, stone, or piece of timber that lies under a door.

Throw valves—Lever-type valves to turn water on and off.

Treads—These are the flat stepping members that the foot steps onto in a stairway.

UV system—A system that uses ultraviolet light to kill or disable bacteria in water.

Vent pipes—These pipes are part of the waste system piping that allows ventilation in the pipes, keeping the water draining quickly and smoothly. Without the ability for air to escape from pipes, the water would drain slowly, toilets would not flush adequately, and clogs would be more likely to occur.

Vermiculite—An early manufactured insulation product.

Vinyl and aluminum siding—A preformed siding that is usually prefinished and requires little or no maintenance.

Wall plates—These are the top or bottom wood members of wall studs.

Waste pipes—Used in the removal of waste water in a building. Pipes can be plastic (ABS or PVC), cast iron, copper, or galvanized steel.

Water heater—A tank that holds hot water generated by either a side-mounted burner, internal burner, or an internal electric element.

Well—Usually a private water source that may be deep-drilled or shallow. A pump is usually installed to deliver the water from the source to the home. An artesian well may not need a pump.

Well expansion tank—A tank that contains the pumped water until it is ready to be used to help create an even flow.

Windowsill—The lower portion of the window that is angled to help water flow off.

XRF paint analyzer—X-ray fluorescence gun; a specialized tool used by professionals to determine the lead content through several layers of paint.

Zone valve—Usually an electric valve used in conjunction with a circulating pump to open or close according to the demands of a thermostat.

Index